The Gift of Simplicity

# The Gift of Simplicity

### June Holland McEwen

**BROADMAN PRESS**
Nashville, Tennessee

Dewey Decimal Classification: 248.5
Subject Heading: CHRISTIAN LIFE
Library of Congress Catalog Card Number: 84-6327
Printed in the United States of America

Unless otherwise noted, all Scripture quotations are taken from the King James Version of the Bible.

All Scripture quotations marked GNB are taken from the *Good News Bible,* the Bible in Today's English Version. Old Testament: Copyright © American Bible Society 1976; New Testament: Copyright © American Bible Society 1966, 1971, 1976. Used by permission.

**Library of Congress Cataloging in Publication Data**

McEwen, June Holland, 1930-
  The gift of simplicity.

  Bibliography: p. 124
  1. Simplicity—Religious aspects—Christianity.
I. Title.
BV4647.S48M37   1984          241'.4     84-6327
ISBN 0-8054-5914-6 (pbk.)

For Jack,
Nell and Tom,
Melanie and Randy,
Jeffrey and Meredith,
because I love you.

4286

'Tis a gift to be simple
'Tis a gift to be free
'Tis a gift to come down
Where you ought to be.
And when you find yourself
In the place just right,
'Twill be in the valley
Of love and delight.

—An Old Shaker Hymn

# Contents

# Introduction

It is important that the reader of this book keep in mind that I do not set myself up as one who has achieved the simplified life-style or as one who has developed the gift of simplicity to any remarkable degree. Rather, the occasion for this book is my own need to reorder priorities, to simplify, to take more control of my time. I need to find more time for prayer, study, and contemplation. Thus the book is a response to my need to search for simplicity and to develop the gift which the Shaker hymn invokes. I am acutely aware of the need to escape from the distress resulting from the complexity caused by my own manner of living.

This work arises from a growing awareness that Christians must make choices about cultural values, perform responsible work on behalf of peace, and become involved in vital issues such as world hunger. Many are farther along in their struggles than I, and I am learning from them.

This present effort to discuss the search is vital. Christians must continually take a serious look at the bondage imposed by the complexity of modern life and society. This complexity inhibits our freedom to grow, to be thoroughly Christian, and to take our places IN the world without being OF the world.

May your reading of these pages cause you to begin your own search, or to continue your struggle with renewed courage, as appropriate to where you are in your own Christian pilgrimage.

# 1

# WHY DO WE SEARCH?

## The Need for Simplicity

At times we all long for the simple life; usually we yearn for the good old days. We have visions of simpler and less complicated ways of living. We dream of an era when folks had more time of their own and less obligations to other people's plans. When we examine our longings for days gone by, we are stunned to realize that those were days of struggle and sacrifice. Often people had less materially and more worry about basic needs and simple safety. Perhaps they were unaware that they were "enjoying" a simple life!

Today many people are bogged down in overscheduled calendars and days of dashing from one event to another. Many families are trying to manage the logistics of dental appointments, piano lessons, dinner meetings, and social engagements. At least, this is the case for most middle-class Americans. They sigh and murmur, "I need to take control. I need some time for myself. I need to simplify my life."

With fleeting moments of wishful thinking and occasional resolutions to do better, we have moments of hope. More often than not, the glimmer fades in the gathering shadows of just making it to the next activity. We take courage and

**11**

try to survive until bedtime. Dropping into exhausted sleep, we wish life *were* more simple.

Anytime anyone manages to achieve some objectives which do simplify, there is a feeling of exultation and joy. "It certainly makes my life less complicated." "It has simplified my life." These announcements are statements of small victories. Congratulations are in order from family and friends.

Faced with busy days, feeling pulled at by demands from all directions, each of us responds with some degree of frustration. We want to have better quality in all our activities. We desire quality time with children, parents, spouses, and friends. Our attention is drawn to the possibility of long walks, watching a sunset, having solitude. We wish for enough time for Bible study, reading a good book, or taking a course at college. Also, it would be satisfying to have time for those who need attention on a regular basis: the elderly, the ill, the lonely.

There is so much good that needs doing and so little disposable time in which to do it. We know of many things we want to do but end up leaving them undone due to lack of time and energy. There is no magic wand to wave to effect these changes. Instead, we are mesmerized by the charming but false hope that tomorrow we will change. Tomorrow we will get our schedules and priorities lined out properly. We shy away from the reality that many important things are accomplished only by determination. Hard decisions must be made.

Determination must be reclaimed again and again. The dieter must diet every day. The athlete must train regularly. The pianist must continue daily practicing. Victories do not stay won; the battleground shifts. We refurbish worn armor, sharpen dull weapons, find the best terrain, and engage again in the battle for today.

This ceaseless effort sounds grim, but it need not be. An attitude toward life can be developed, an attitude charged with joy. We can divide up the big battles into winnable smaller skirmishes. Setting our sights on the manageable, we can perform today's task with gladness. A deep sense of satisfaction will be one result.

Simplicity and a sense of well-being will come with doing better quality on less quantity of tasks. We must believe that this can be done and that life can be lived simply and joyfully. The simple life does not mean a return to the mythical "good old days." Our coping with the pain, loss, and sorrow which is integral to human experience will be more successful if we have the preparation of a simple life-style. We will endure the hard times by taking them as they come. Then we will claim Jesus' assurance, "Sufficient unto the day is the evil thereof" (Matt. 6:34).

Elton Trueblood, the great Quaker minister-teacher, observes that the fundamental nature of simple living is a requirement of the gospel of Jesus Christ. However, Trueblood says:

> We are not likely to be satisfied with a simpler standard of living unless we have found inner peace which eliminates the constant struggle to possess more things. Much of the hectic nature of contemporary living arises from the constant escalation of ambition to possess, the terrible fact being that possessiveness is, by its intrinsic nature, insatiable. The man with a million dollars, far from being satisfied, wants more. The solution of this problem will come, if it comes at all, not by acquiring more, but

by finding an inner peace which renders the hectic pace unnecessary.[1]

To find inner peace and reduce the pace we must make changes. Facing up to reorganizing and simplifying means giving attention to our desires. An honest look at what we *want* and what we *need* will help to properly order priorities. Certainly we are right to see to basic needs: food, shelter, clothing, and health care. But at the same time our need for inner peace and self-control must be given attention. We seek financial security and a stable and peaceful society. We hope our children will adopt our values and pass them on.

The hungry must be fed and other needs of our neighbors attended to. Having communities where crime is deterred and the criminal reformed is a legitimate dream. We want jobs, security against disabilities, provision for old age, and proper education for the young. We ache for appreciation, encouragement, and love. We long for prestige, importance, and admiration. In the face of all this mixture, we need a community of faith for support and for a vehicle to give meaning and purpose for living. To find inner peace is not easy. Developing the gift of simplicity is a way to begin.

When considering what we want and what we need, we are forced to look at what we have. How do we balance these three? Certainly there is an amazing complexity in just the use of time, let alone in the vast area of human relationships. In modern political processes and in the field of economics there is bewilderment and a constant cliff-hanging threat of chaos and failure. International affairs seem to teeter on the edge of calamity. In the face of such monumental uncertainties people are made ill by these pressures and stresses under which we live.

Too often individuals feel helpless to shape events or even to control the course of their own lives. Giant corporations, big government, large institutions loom over the smaller units of family, friends, and church. Life is darkened by personal problems which are compounded by guilt, anxiety, and fear. Dealings with others are clouded by resentment, envy, and jealousy. People carry burdens and worries like Christian in *The Pilgrim's Progress.* Many times we, like Bunyan's Christian, find ourselves sinking into all kinds of sloughs of worry and despondency. Too often our spiritual lives are barren, without joy, without vitality, without growth.

In the face of such a dreary picture, it is well to observe those among us who have found a way of living that gives them strength for trials, joy for everyday living, and motivation to serve God and others. These persons give evidence of spiritual growth by their simple living and maturity. We are in need of this gift of simple living, "the gift to come down/Where we ought to be." Some are aware of the need; some are not. The gift lies within waiting to be recognized and developed. This search and discovery will ensure that we will "find ourselves/In the place just right,/'Twill be in the valley/Of love and delight."

What better place? To love one another, showing forth that we are Christ's disciples, is surely a delectable valley. To delight in the Word and in keeping God's commandments is a valley of peace and of joy unspeakable.

A look at a few families caught in life-style dilemmas will illustrate why we need to engage in such a search and why there is reward for simplicity in living.

The clock's alarm rings delicately but insistently. James begins to surface groggily from his lagoon of sleep. He

gropes for the button shutting out the sound. Diving back
into the warm bedcovers, he waits. Before his mind's eye
looms the possibility of floating back into the waves of drow-
siness. Today is Sunday. The knowledge of the day of the
week brings him to alertness. He throws back the sheets
and steps firmly into preparations for the busiest and best
day of the week.

Sunday. For this family of five, the day is tightly sched-
uled. A quick breakfast of cereal, juice, and coffee is followed
by a scramble for study materials and Bibles. Everyone
dashes to the car and is whisked away to the church. For the
most part, the rush and dash are friendly and cooperative,
although there are some tensions. Occasional sharp words
erupt but are nipped quickly by a firm word from the parents.

After church school and morning worship, the Prince
family stops at a fast-food restaurant. Here they gobble
down fish, fries, slaw, and iced tea before going home. Once
there, they read the Sunday paper, change clothes, and
coordinate schedules for the rest of the day. Transportation
is arranged for James' and Leanne's committee meetings at
the church. Jeff and Lisa need to be on time for youth choir.
Homework and playtime are arranged for eight-year-old
Sandra. The entire family plans to be back together for
evening worship. There will be recreation afterward as well
as time for coffee and good talk with friends.

A hectic day—Sunday—a day of rest! On the remaining
days of the week the family scatters for jobs, school, social
life. Each one participates in midweek church, sports
events, activities with friends, and community service. One
theme running through everyday is the multitude of concerns with paying bills and seeing to needs of others. At

various times, different ones are involved in large and small celebrations. The Prince family members are middle-class Americans living the good life.

Material needs for all the family are met without too much thought. In Abraham Maslow's hierarchy of needs, these people are well into levels of fulfilling matters of mind and spirit, beyond giving most attention to basic survival needs.

Yet, each one has some puzzling feelings of dissatisfactions. Each experiences times of aimlessness, boredom, even occasional depression. Odd emotions for people who are so well off. A contemporary novelist and philosopher comments on just such attitudes. He asks a series of probing questions about a man in New York:

> Why is it that a man riding a good commuter train from Larchmont to New York, whose needs and drives are satisfied, who has a good home, loving wife and family, good job, who enjoys unprecedented "cultural and recreational facilities," often feels bad without knowing why?[2]

One response to these questions for Christians today is to make their own individual litany of questions. To ask questions is the first step; questions define the problem. As Christians they often are in bondage, struggling with the complexities of modern affluent life-styles. This litany can include:

Why do Christian families often operate in an atmosphere of impatience and irritability?

Why do Christian families feel pressured to add to their material possessions?

Why do they feel trapped by a spirit of need for more and more things?

Why are Christian families oppressed by bad money management?

Why are there too many bills to pay, too little savings, too little to give away to others?

Why do Christian families overschedule their time?

Why do they leave little time for prayer?

Why is there no time for solitude, meditation, and contemplation in the lives of most people today?

Why do Christian families succumb to burnout, stress reactions, and broken relationships?

Why is there inadequate communication, too much anger and guilt?

Why are Christians burdened down by resentment, anxiety, worry, and depression?

Why are Christians nearly powerless on issues such as the quality of movies, books, and drama?

Why are they deluged by effects of advertisement in so many of the daily choices they make?

Why are Christians affected more and more by popular cultural value systems?

Why are Christians increasingly traumatized by the reports on the nightly news on television?

Why are Christian families so often torn between opinions and courses of action?

Why is there little or no interest in participation in politics and social action?

Why are Christians confused by the rising tide of religious cults in the country?

Why are Christians frightened by the sweeping up of thousands of youth into non-Christian ideologies?

Why are many Christian families lacking in clear-cut moral values?

Why are they confused by current alternative living arrangements?

How can Christians cope with increasing tolerance of nonbiblical ways of living?

How are Christians to cope with the increasing indulgence for the individual at the cost of the best interest of the community?

All these and other questions point out that life today *is* complex. We are bound to do so many things over which we seem to have little choice or control. How can a Christian family entertain the *idea,* let alone the *actions,* needed to simplify their lives? How can they begin to develop the nearly lost gift of simple living? How can Christians move toward freedom from the bondage imposed by modern life and by its myriad complexities? After all, few people desire and even fewer are willing to deliberately lower their standard of living.

When confronted with the proposal that Christians should develop the gift of simple living, one woman became angry. She wondered if this meant living like her grandmother. "My grandmother worked hard all morning in the kitchen to get meals on the table. I can get a good meal ready in minutes. Do you mean I must go back to the old ways of cooking?" No. That is NOT the idea. To live simply, to develop the gift of simplicity, is not to go back. It is not to stop progress.

One proponent of the simple life states very clearly the case for both progress and simplicity:

> The simplification of our lives should not be equated with turning away from progress. To the contrary, simplicity is crucial for progress, for without simplicity we will be

overwhelmed by massive social and material complexity. To simplify is to bring order, clarity, and purpose to our lives. These qualities are not opposed to progress; rather they are crucial foundations for progress.[3]

Simplicity will bring new growth to society, and the resulting growth will be both material and spiritual. This kind of growth will benefit the present society by bringing progress of a kind desperately needed.

We do not spend hours of labor on many of the tasks that took so much time for our grandparents. But what have we done with the hours gained by labor-saving devices? Perhaps we have dedicated much of the salvaged time to activity for activity's sake. Each of us can make a long list of clubs, committees, shopping trips, entertainments, and other activities which take our time. These countless hours of busyness restrict our freedom. Our priorities seem to be set without much deliberate choice. We are so involved that we have little time left for developing ourselves in the realms of spirit, intellect, and emotions.

It goes without saying that human beings long for wealth, possessions, fame, and prestige. The reasons for setting priorities in these areas are many and varied. Human beings desire to have control of self, others, and events. Human beings apparently must be reassured about their own importance. There is a widespread if not universal longing to be unique. People want to be secure, to be needed, to be admired, to be important.

Perhaps a review of these desires can make us aware that these longings are elemental and universal. To keep these needs in a proper balance, it is well to take a long look at the way we live. A study of the Scriptures will reveal the

principles of Christian living and aid in developing the gift
of simplicity. A simple manner of living can be achieved if
we are willing to learn from the example of Jesus.

Jesus reminded us, "Take heed, and beware of covetousness: for a man's life consisteth not in the abundance of
things which he possesseth" (Luke 12:15). The writer of
Hebrews said, "Keep your lives free from the love of money,
and be satisfied with what you have. For God has said, 'I will
never leave you; I will never abandon you' " (Heb. 13:5,
GNB).

To be content one needs sufficient food, clothing, shelter,
and health care. Life is enjoyable with enough strength and
health. Living is made meaningful by work. Life is pleasura-
ble when we have a sense of purpose, the knowledge of being
needed, and the awareness of our importance to others.

What kinds of situations require Christians to struggle to
find a simple way of living? Let's look at some instances
which bring into focus the need to develop the gift of simplicity.

Collecting a book, the crossword puzzle, and a sharp pen-
cil, Ruth settled herself into the recliner. Sipping the fresh-
ly brewed coffee, she hardly listened to the soundtrack of
voices provided by the television across the room. As she
tried to think of a word for *swamp denizen,* her ears picked
up a tone of desperate appeal coming from the TV. Looking
up, she saw that the picture on the tube was of little children with large eyes and skinny limbs and distended bellies.
Her heart ached; her conscience groaned; her mind
searched for a course of action.

Ruth is retired and her income is adequate for her needs.
She does have some discretionary funds in her limited budg-

et. Ruth would like to respond to the hungry children she has just seen on the television.

Steve is recently out of college but still living at home. He is one of many young Americans searching for a job. He needs a place to begin his career. He needs a car, clothes, expense money for his job search. Driving into the city for interviews, he passes through blocks of slums. He is sensitive to the plight of the people living in miserable houses with poorly fed children and unemployed young people standing about. His own keen need for work makes him sympathize with them all.

Rick is looking for part-time summer work. He has a small scholarship for his third year of college. The pressure is on to save money for the fall semester. He sees elderly people in his community who are hard put to have enough electricity to keep cool. Income is limited and their expenses keep rising. Rick is touched by their struggles.

Reed is aware of the needs of people in his community and the needs of others in faraway places. He is a policeman and a deacon in the church. He must support his family of a wife and four children on a limited income. Each week his pastor points out the need to give regularly to the church and to worldwide missions. Reed struggles to be a responsible steward of his resources. He has a difficult time being responsible for all the causes he holds dear.

Carol is an associational denominational employee. Her work is satisfying. As a church worker, her pay is not at all overly generous. Recently married, she wonders how she will be able to furnish her small apartment, attend night classes, and give to others as she would like.

Like Ruth, Steve, Rick, Reed, and Carol, we are all limited in what we can do and in how much time we can allot to others. These limitations and restrictions bind us just as surely as earlier generations were bound. Where they spent long hours to provide the basics, we spend time to gain things, possessions, power, and prestige. Too often the desire for these things is determined for us by forces outside ourselves. We are freed from devoting time to labor-intensive activities only to become bound by desires for things. We give up control of our lives, our time, our values to fulfill many desires not of our own choosing.

To combat this situation, we must decide who is in charge. We must choose a way of simplicity and reject a life of complexity.

Who sets our priorities? Who decides what is of value? Where we go, how we spend time and money, what we read, where we use energy is ours to decide. On what basis do we make decisions about clothing, cars, housing, voting, living? How we choose and what we choose is a Christian responsibility.

We must look afresh at the principles set forth in the Bible. Let us look to the life of Christ and reconsider him as our model. Once these principles and his example are before us, we can set about developing the gift of simplicity. Setting personal goals and planning a manner of living in keeping with Christian principles becomes a real alternative. By turning to the Bible we can commence the search for rules of simple living which aid in developing the gift of simplicity.

# Notes

1. Elton Trueblood, *Quarterly Yoke Letter,* vol. 22 (Dec. 1980), no. 4, p. 1.

2. Walker Percy, *The Message in the Bottle* (New York: Farrar, Straus and Giroux, 1980), p. 4.

3. Duane Elgin, *Voluntary Simplicity* (New York: William Morrow, 1981), p. 37.

# 2

# REASONS FOR THE SEARCH

## The Biblical Basis for Simple Living

The basic characteristics in Christian living involve discipline, creative simplicity, and freedom. To consciously choose the discipline of simplicity, to whatever degree, is to decide to move from a standard of success based on achievement and accumulation to a standard of spiritual growth based on the worth of persons—persons for whom Christ died.

To shift our standards for success is not easy. To live even a little of our lives in creatively simple styles is beset with difficulty. We need to ask, "What are some features of life today that make our lives so complex?" Most of us will agree that it is difficult to live a creatively simple life in our culture today. So many things make life complex.

A small voice deep within us poses questions hard to answer. "What size and how heavy is that pack on your back? How heavily does the burden of your use of time and money weigh you down? Are you carrying the load imposed by today's headlines and the lead stories of the six o'clock news?

"Are you bowed down by coping with cultural changes in

25

marriage, divorce, abortion, living together, success and failure, materialism and hedonism—changes which impinge on your family, your church, your community? Are you overwhelmed by the array of choices put before you in the areas of religion, politics, economics?

"Do you consciously *know* that you can exercise control over the amount of weight you carry in your backpack? Do you know that Jesus and the Bible speak to these choices?

"Are you traveling light, or are you slowly sinking beneath an intolerably complex, heavy load?" In response we ask, "What does *simplicity* mean in a Christian's life-style?" *Life-style* is a relatively new word; what does it mean? One writer states:

> At its most basic level, human life is organized around the acquisition of food, affection, shelter, clothing, and health care. Around these basic human needs are the basic "means" through which these needs are met: employment, transportation, education, recreation, and celebration. *Life-style is the manner in which persons go about meeting their needs.* It includes that blend of tastes, habits, and practices which characterize a person's everyday behavior and relationships.[1]

If *life-style* means "the manner in which persons go about meeting their needs," it is immediately apparent that the Christian pilgrim needs to give serious attention to his or her life-style. Realizing that modern life has become increasingly complex, we must give attention to deliberately choosing simplicity in our Christian life-style.

*Simplicity* is the opposite of *complexity.* Webster uses as synonyms for *simplicity* such words as *innocence, candor, clarity, plainness;* for *complexity* a statement which does not really define: "the quality or state of being complex." Perhaps simplicity of life-style needs amplification from a Christian who has practiced it. Elton Trueblood, the contemporary Quaker minister-teacher, has written:

> I know that we must strive consistently to find the real priority of our lives and let the consequences take care of themselves. The real priority, I have long believed, is to seek first the kingdom of God (Luke 12:31). Emphasis on a magnificent "yes" will give courage to utter "no" when simplicity requires it.[2]

Richard Foster, another Quaker, has ten controlling principles to aid in learning the discipline of simplicity. The ten principles are as follows:

1. Buy things for their usefulness rather than their status.
2. Reject anything that is producing an addiction in you.
3. Develop a habit of giving things away.
4. Refuse to be propagandized by the custodians of modern gadgetry.
5. Learn to enjoy things without owning them.
6. Develop a deeper appreciation for creation.
7. Look with a healthy skepticism at all "buy now, pay later" schemes.
8. Obey Jesus' instructions about plain, honest speech.
9. Reject anything that will breed the oppression of others.
10. Shun whatever would distract you from your main goal.[3]

These principles are worthy of thought, consideration, observation, and application.

There are many ways to begin to live more simply; there are ways to do so in creative modes suitable for each person. No hard, set rules, no absolute formulae are the *only* way. There is a challenge for each of us to decide on how to develop the gift of simplicity which is possible for us. The extent of the simplicity is an individual choice. We may become more involved in simple living in certain stages of life and/or in particular areas of living. The important thing is to start the search, engage in the struggle.

A move toward simplicity is a move toward freedom and more control of one's own life. Meeting basic needs in a more responsible Christian manner is a step to inner satisfaction and effective outer witnessing.

Creative simplicity is a means to fulfillment of Jesus' command that we love one another. Simple living is a way to demonstrate our discipleship. In such simplicity we will

> share our affluence,
> conserve our planet,
> grow through prayer and solitude,
> enjoy fellowship and friendship,
> spend time with family,
> serve others, and
> glorify God by it all.

A Texan named Art epitomizes a life of Christian simplicity. We can learn from him how to develop our own gift.

He was slender to the point of being gaunt and his stooped frame belied his years, making him appear far older than his age of fifty. His sparse, sandy hair seemed always to need smoothing and he wore his Sunday suit self-consciously. You knew he would be more at ease in his brown work pants and checked shirt. His shyness made it difficult to sustain a meeting of the eyes, and this reticence was the reason he could not lead in public prayer even in the small, plain Texas congregation of working people.

Art delivered ice back in World War II days when refrigerators were unobtainable. His hard work and canny ability to ferret out opportunities that turned a healthy profit allowed his family to live well. He had the quiet respect of bankers and merchants in the small cotton farm community and county seat town.

His family adored him and listened to and acted on his rarely given advice and opinions. His church elected him a deacon. His grandchildren knew they were safe in the center of his huge heart and his unflinching attention. Even the stray cats knew they could count on a generous helping from the bags of commercial cat food stored in his garage just for them.

Art is hardly a classic example of what most of us would describe as a *saint* or *model Christian*. We tend to visualize more dramatic and romantic people as saints and holy men. For me, however, Art Smith represents the best in a follower of Jesus of Nazareth; he exemplifies the man who bears the fruits of the spirit: joy, love, peace, patience, kindness, goodness, faithfulness, humility, and self-control.

Art is one of the best Christians I have known. How about you? Reflect for a moment and see whose image comes to mind when you ask yourself, "Who is the best Christian I have ever known?" With this person fixed on the screen of your consciousness, ask yourself, "Why do I consider this person an exemplary follower of Christ? What did she/he do, say, or how behave, or demonstrate an attitude or spirit that makes me apply the description—best Christian?"

There are several Scripture passages which outline similar characteristics and are the standards for evaluation and recognition of the fruits of the Spirit in persons who are examples of Jesus Christ.

## CHARACTERISTIC BEHAVIOR IF ONE LIVES BY THE TEN COMMANDMENTS

God spoke in Exodus 20, GNB:

1. Worship no God but me.
2. Do not make for yourselves images. (Do not bow down to any idol.)
3. Do not use my name for evil purposes.
4. Observe the sabbath and keep it holy.
5. Respect your father and your mother.
6. Do not commit murder.
7. Do not commit adultery.
8. Do not steal.
9. Do not accuse anyone falsely.
10. Do not desire another's possessions.

The best Christians I have known across the years are people who have obeyed these commands and whose conduct and attitudes reveal their determination to live according to these precepts.

It somehow seems out of fashion today to desire to be a good person. Our culture causes us to "look out for No. 1," to learn to "pull our own strings," to be successful, rich, slim, fulfilled—anything and everything except to be a *good person*. The Christian can and should decide that to be a good person, a good Christian, is an acceptable and desirable goal.

## THE CHARACTERISTICS OF ACCEPTANCE OF OUR HUMAN LIMITS

Job protested his innocence and insisted he did not deserve the misfortunes which had befallen him. He kept asking, "Why?"

God answered him out of the storm: "Job, you challenged Almighty God;/will you give up now, or will you answer?" (40:1-2, GNB).

"Are you trying to prove that I am unjust—/to put me in the wrong and yourself in the right?" (40:8, GNB).

Then Job answered the Lord. "I know, Lord, that you are all-powerful;/that you can do everything you want." (42:2, GNB).

## THE CHARACTERISTICS REQUIRED BY GOD

The Christian should have the characteristics of JUSTICE, MERCY, HUMILITY; THESE ARE CHARACTERISTICS REQUIRED BY GOD. "The Lord has told us what is good. What he requires of us is this: to do what is just, to show constant love, and to live in humble fellowship with our God" (Mic. 6:8, GNB).

It has been said we all *deserve* justice but we plead for *mercy*. Sometimes we insist on justice being meted out to others while reserving mercy, tolerance, and understanding for ourselves. For example, how does the Christian community treat a minister with an alcohol problem? Do we forgive and help or do we fire him? How do we relate to an unwed mother? What do we do for a deacon arrested for drunk driving?

## THE CHARACTERISTICS OF A HAPPY PERSON

In the Sermon on the Mount Jesus described the person who is truly happy.

Happy are those

"who are spiritually poor
who mourn
who are humble
whose greatest desire is to do what God requires
who are merciful to others
who are pure in heart
who work for peace
who are persecuted
who are insulted, lied against for being Jesus' followers.
Be happy and glad, for a great reward is kept for you in
heaven" (Matt. 5:12, GNB).

These are hardly characteristics one would find in a current magazine's lead article on how to be happy, but they deserve our careful study.

## THE CHARACTERISTICS OF A DISCIPLE

Not long before his death, Jesus gave a final commandment to his followers. This command prescribes specific behavior for his disciples.

Jesus said, "And now I give you a new commandment: love one another. As I have loved you, so you must love one another. If you have love for one another, then everyone will know that you are my disciples" (John 13:34-35, GNB).

M. Scott Peck in his book, *The Road Less Traveled,* defines love in an interesting way. He says that love is the spiritual nurture of another, and that is an act of the will, an action requiring courage, discipline, and sometimes suffering.[4]

Think of *love* as you think of elderly parents and your responsibility, or rebellious children, demanding spouse, or other hard tasks requiring courage and discipline to act in a *loving*, Christian manner.

## THE CHARACTERISTICS OF ACTION

*"Do not deceive yourselves by just listening to his word; instead, put it into practice.* Whoever listens to the word but does not put it into practice is like a man who looks in a mirror and sees himself as he is. He takes a good look at himself and then goes away and at once forgets what he looks like. *But whoever looks closely into the perfect law that sets people free, who keeps on paying attention to it and does not simply listen and then forget it, but puts it into practice —that person will be blessed by God in what he does."* (Jas. 1:22-25, GNB, italics added).

The Word, the Perfect Law, our sterling example, is Jesus of Nazareth. We are under orders to act out the imperatives of the good news embodied in the life and teachings of the gentle Galilean. Review in your mind's eye Jesus' relationships, his caring, healing, and teaching, his praying, his dying, and his resurrection. Jesus is our example. We are obliged to be like him.

As we have examined these Bible passages, images of Christians of all ages, every position, varying degrees of education and culture, small/great success, and of every level of education have flitted across the screens of our recollections.

Each of us has our personal Hall of Heroes and Heroines —people who remind us by their lives of the strong and gentle Jesus of long ago who is still present among us through them. We see in them this one who himself was full

of love, joy, peace, patience, kindness, goodness, faithfulness, humility, and self-control. This man owned only the
robe he wore, yet he changed the world. Christians who
have the gift of simplicity and emulate the qualities of Jesus
Christ also show forth fruits of the spirit. Their simplicity
is a gift which testifies of him and which revolutionizes the
society in which they live.

# Notes

1. Davis Cream and Eric and Helen Ebbeson, *Living Simply: An Examination of Christian Lifestyles* (New York: The Seabury Press, 1981), p. 11.

2. Elton Trueblood, *Quarterly Yoke Letter,* vol. 22 (Dec. 1980), no. 4, p. 2.

3. Ibid.

4. M. Scott Peck, *The Road Less Traveled* (New York: Simon & Schuster, 1978), p. 119.

# 3

# OBSTACLES TO THE SEARCH

## Causes of Complexity

On the surface it seems every thoughtful Christian surely would choose to live simply. But if we look at ourselves and those we know well, it is immediately apparent that few actually practice simple living. What causes life to be so complex and simplicity so difficult? What are the obstacles that prevent exercise of the gift of simplicity?

A good deal of the root of complexity in American life is the result of American standards of success. We are subjected to a constant barrage of advertising by means of all the media dramatizing for us what it means to be successful. We are told that to be successful by these standards is to be happy. From automobiles to personal grooming articles, we are assured that the access to these products, their use, their display, their possession will mark us as having it made.

A cursory glance in the mall book stores reveals a large section of self-help books which promise speedy moves up the ladder of success. The cover of most popular magazines indicate at least one article promising to show the reader how to overcome some defect or play up some attribute which will unerringly lead to a higher level of success. These ideas range from making friends to choosing appropriate colors for one's wardrobe.

Our literature, both popular and serious, is filled with characters who start from the lowest levels of society and move to the top. Hard work, sparkling personality, incredible good fortune, and just being American assures these characters happy endings to their adventures.

From Horatio Alger's time (1834–1899; he wrote over one hundred stories for boys. The hero of his novels was an exemplary boy struggling against great odds who gains wealth, fame, and honor by dent of hard work)[1] until today's success stories of TV's *Dallas* and *Dynasty,* wealth and power are the marks of achievement. It is interesting to note that Alger's heroes valued honesty, integrity, and honor—values given short shrift in the power plays of the twentieth century oil tycoon or Wall Street wizard, featured in soap operas, movies, and novels.

For Americans the stuff of everyday life is competition, beating others out, being number 1, getting ahead of the Joneses, upward mobility in both social class and economic class. The metaphor inherent in our culture's fascination with the violence and the competition in football has been described enough that it needs only a mention here. Competition is an unexamined but socially acceptable attitude. If one really took a hard look at everything involved in competition, it would be hard to support this extreme attitude as being in the spirit of Christ. The very suggestion of criticizing the competitive spirit in American society evokes strong arguments in defense of the virtues it engenders. The feelings are so strong that it is almost impossible to have a thoughtful discussion. How about you as you read these words? Do you find yourself resisting and thinking of reasons for encouraging competitiveness? A look at 1 Corinthians 13 with competition in mind will give food for some deep thought.

Another root of complexity and an obstacle to the simple life is our tendency to confuse needs and wants. These ideas have been commented on in an early chapter. Suffice it to say at this point that a clear view of the difference between wants and needs and goals set with the difference in mind will result in progress toward simpler living.

In the same vein, another obstacle in the way of developing the gift of simplicity is the modern emphasis on the rights of the individual. This individualism-gone-wild is seen in titles of best-selling books such as *Pulling Your Own Strings* and *Looking Out for No. 1*. Sociologists have labeled this era as the "Me Generation." An often-heard response to moral questions is, "If it feels good, it's all right." Hedonism is not restricted to the ancient world; it is very much alive in many parts of American culture. Self-centeredness, selfishness, and ego enhancement have been elevated to not only respectable levels but to desirable and necessary modes of behavior. Today's youth are often puzzled at missionary volunteers, Peace Corps participants, and others willing to give themselves for the good of others.

This self-centeredness is shortsighted in one particularly dreadful way. Using up the resources of the environment, making enormous piles of hazardous waste, and piling up huge federal deficits show a criminal disregard for future generations. Too often we have interpreted God's command to Adam and Eve to dress the earth as a license to exploit the planet without any thought to those who will come after us.

Also, as another obstacle, we must admit that human beings enjoy creature comforts and thrive on increasing levels of easy living. Luxury is satisfying. It is pleasant to indulge oneself. At times in the history of many societies, the government has seen this human inclination as a threat to the peace and prosperity of the realm.

To control expenditures on luxuries, sumptuary laws were set forth by rulers or enacted by parliaments. These laws limited the amount of money which citizens could spend on private luxuries. An example is the law passed by the English Parliament during the reign of Edward III (1327-1377) restricting the number of courses of a meal to two except on holidays. "The term [sumptuary] originally denoted regulations restricting extravagance in food, drink, dress and household equipment, usually for religious or moral reasons."[2]

This is not to suggest enactment of such laws today but to illustrate that a taste for luxury is universal. Efforts to control indulgence are as old as the race—by law, by religious teaching, and by personal discipline. It is an area still demanding attention!

The complexities of modern American life are so well known that one hesitates to present the litany once again. Thoughtful evaluation of these factors will supply a clue for each person to find a place in his/her own life to take hold in order to devise some plan for simplifying.

The sheer number of people in our land is a definite cause of complexity. The increase in population affects how much attention persons can expect in marketing, education, health care, and other areas which require service from organizations and institutions.

Today's trend toward nuclear families and the increase in

one-parent households make dealing with life's challenges more complex. In the past the extended family offered help in care of children and in providing for the elderly. There was emotional and moral support in being in a situation surrounded by many kinfolk which is too often missing for today's small family. Celebrations and traditions suffer also as families decrease in size and increase in isolation.

Connected to the smaller family is the American penchant for moving about. This mobility is doubtless an aid for job search and for taking advantage of opportunities. The greatest casualty of constant mobility is the rootedness and sense of place which gives people strong identity. Often families feel this lack most severely as children reach the crisis of adolescence and have need for a safe environment in which to test their own beliefs. The strong mores of place and family and the solidity of knowing one's roots can often be of immeasurable assistance to the young person searching for his/her own identity.

Another part of life which adds to the complexity of today's people is in the work we do. With increasing specialization and greater assembly-line kinds of labor, people lose the identity that comes with a vocation. To have pride in one's work is important to self-acceptance and self-esteem. Children often have little idea of what kind of work Mom and Dad perform. It is hard for our youth to learn to have respect for the world of work and for the accomplishments of parents simply because they do not know what kind of work is done. It is difficult to convey to them the value and importance of the labor and time committed by parents to their jobs.

Complexity is well represented by the bigness of modern-day government, corporations, educational institutions, businesses, and many churches. There is rarely any way that huge institutions can deal in simple, close, warm terms with individuals. The large institution has its rules which make the successful operation possible and profitable. The individual must follow procedures to get the service needed.

These and other modern complexities lead to increasing depersonalization. Everyone admits the advantages and the benefits as well as the necessity of moving on into the age of the computer and of increased technology. It is with deep regret that we see as an accompanying feature the lack of personal importance and the decrease in personal attention. These factors contribute to some hopeful signs that people insist on being seen as individuals. Among these signs are the increase in numbers of people who are learning various crafts. The crafts, whether needlework, woodwork, or pottery, make it possible for persons to create and to possess items which are not assembly-line identical. The creative outlet is surely immensely satisfying to the craftsman.

Modern affluence leads to some of the obstacles to simple living. Christians need to read again the preaching of Old Testament prophets against the rich who have obtained wealth by exploiting the poor. We must guard against labeling all poor people as lazy and ineffectual. One observation about the poor to keep before us is the New Testament statement that the poor heard Jesus gladly. How often the missionary efforts of Christians are aimed at and are most fruitful among the poor and the outcast!

Sometimes affluent Christians are caught in the paradoxical position of searching for a religious reason for being rich. There is a terrible temptation to reason that one must be righteous, else why would God shower one with such good fortune. We have yet to fully learn the lesson taught by the Book of Job. Some of God's brightest saints have had the least of this world's riches. Jesus warned of the great difficulties that come with being rich. Christians explain away or ignore his warnings at great peril. This area of how to act when one has great possessions warrants careful and extended study by church members today. We tread on dangerous ground when we apply standards of success dictated by the world rather than standards set forth in the Bible.

We have heard the example of how Americans use the majority of the world's resources on their small proportion of the world's population. We see in the daily news reports arguments about using up natural resources such as oil, coal, pure water, and clean air. Occasionally the full impact of what we are doing and how we are depriving generations of the future is driven home. We are shocked by the drama of a Times Beach, Missouri. Lines for suddenly short supplies of gasoline make us realize that the reserves of petroleum will not last indefinitely. Feature stories about irrigation sapping the midwestern watertables scare us for a moment.

We read of lakes and rivers which have been killed by waste disposal. It is encouraging to see associations formed, people mobilized to bring back to life a Lake Erie or a Hudson River. Such successes indicate what can be done when people decide to act. The serious Christian and the responsible citizen need to become informed and to find proper means of action to protect the planet which is our home.

Probably the most defeating element in all this modern maze is the prevalent feeling that one person can do nothing. This sense of helplessness is the root of the apathy and indifference which stalks the land. A move to simplicity, to valuing the basic needs for living, to lessening demands for more and more things is an antidote and effective resistance to the careless consumption of resources which rightfully belong to future earth dwellers.

Not only should we be careful stewards for benefit of future generations, but we need to critically analyze how we take the lion's share today. What is our responsibility to the populations of crowded and poor Third World countries? Can we continue to send our missionaries to preach the gospel without some concrete demonstrations of sharing what we have in material abundance? It is a cliché to say that you cannot win a hungry man to Christ; you must feed him first so that he can have the ability to listen and to think about his eternal soul. To share in this manner will take massive, planned action on the part of all Americans. Surely the Christians in the land can be the leaven to effect changes in attitudes and in public policy so that sharing in a real and effective manner can be accomplished.

A first step for an individual is to resolve to use less, to waste less, to share more. There are many avenues open for such actions. To seek these avenues alone or in groups will lessen the obstacles to concrete achievements. The obstacles are all about us. It is not easy to go against the popular life-style. People are angered when their way of living is questioned, regardless of how sincere the questioner is. Moves in the direction of simplicity are bound to be opposed. Opposition will take peculiar forms and will come from surprising sources.

Some thoughtful people have proposed that society be based on having things primarily for utilitatian purposes only. Others will argue that items and objects of beauty must be allowed; beauty is a necessity for a fully human existence. Shakers and Quakers in our own history have managed to do both: to create things of utility which are also things of beauty. The important thing is for Christians to think, to discuss, to take a reasoned approach to choices and commitments.

There are many causes of complexity and many obstacles to a Christian pursuing a mode of life characterized by simplicity. One other cause to consider in this not at all definitive list is the barrier we erect for ourselves. This barrier is of our own making when we allow other people or other events to control our lives, to make decisions for us, to set the criteria by which we judge ourselves.

Our time is taken up by doing things that others consider important. How often do you and your family sit down, perhaps at the beginning of a new year, and take a survey of what you do with your time? Have you learned to say a firm, polite no to the two or three extra responsibilities that overload your calendar? Do you have the courage to set aside quiet time, time with no structured activity? You might ask yourself, "Who is in charge, anyway?"

Often we let runaway emotions and harmful relationships complicate our lives to such an extent that we feel trapped and powerless. A later chapter examines these complexities.

In conclusion, it is safe to say that if we identify the obstacles and the causes of complexity in our living, we have taken a first step to dealing with them in a positive way. A positive approach will aid in the search for simplicity and in developing the gift which lies within us. After all, Jesus commanded us to "Seek . . . first the kingdom of God, and his righteousness; and all these things shall be added unto you" (Matt. 6:33).

## Notes

1. Ida Jayne Hoye, "The Legacy of Horatio Alger," *The Chattanooga News-Free Press* (Dec. 4, 1983), p. J-7.

2. "Sumptuary Laws," *The New Encyclopedia Britannica,* vol. 9 (Chicago: Encyclopedia Britannica, Inc., 1983), p. 669.

# 4

# THE SEARCH FOR SATISFACTION

## Roots of Bondage in Attitudes Toward Money and Possessions

Human beings often act on the false assumption that satisfaction can be found in possessions. We ignore well-publicized examples of tragic unhappiness such as multimillionaire Howard Hughes. If Christians develop and cultivate a right attitude toward possessions, the result will be a more simple, more relaxed, and more enjoyable life-style.

In 1899 Edward A. Grubbs defined the simple life as being characterized by fewness of wants and reasonableness of wants. He said that the opposite of a simple life is one "that cannot be supported without the varied labours of large numbers of other people being directed, in whole or in part, to the satisfaction of its wants. A simple life . . . is one that makes few demands for its support upon the labour of others."[1] Grubbs described reasonableness of wants: "Those wants are reasonable which tend to *health* on all sides of our nature, and whose gratification does not involve a disproportionate sacrifice of other people's labour."[2]

Such simple living does not banish beauty as some might suppose. Beauty ought to be part of simple living. Grubbs insists that "the desire for beauty in all its forms—in dress, in architecture and house-furniture, in wall decoration" is healthy, desirable, and needed.[3]

There are advantages for the Christian in developing simple tastes, not the least of which is saving money. When we think of money, few of us really make the connection that the dollars in our hand represent the hours of labor we have invested in earning it. Of course, the philosophical and political meaning of money as an exchange for labor is a topic in itself. The question of profits is much debated in economic theory. These and related matters are causes of intense debate and tension between the economic systems of capitalism and socialism. Christians need to study and to be aware of such things, but for our consideration we will concentrate on day-to-day uses of money in everyday living.

It is not the purpose here to debate economic theory. But it is imperative that Christians examine the attitudes we hold toward money and toward the accumulation of possessions. The Declaration of Independence states that all men have the right to pursue happiness; it is widely held that the original word used here was not *happiness* but *wealth*. In this connection a modern economist has addressed the subject, "Does Money Buy Happiness?" Richard A. Easterlin observes that happiness is defined both within and among countries as the personal concern with economic matters, family considerations, and health. He notes that of these three, economic concern is most frequently cited. His study reveals that "the satisfaction one gets from his material situation depends not on the absolute of goods he has, but on how this amount compares with what he thinks he needs."[4] It is important to note that he states that "what people perceive as their needs is socially determined."[5]

Easterlin then concludes:

> In general, then, the reason why higher income from a
> society does not typically mean more happiness is that
> the general level of needs, relative to which material
> well-being is judged, grows along with and as a result of
> income growth in the society.[6]

There is danger that Christians will unwittingly slip into
erroneous attitudes which reflect measuring by the wrong
standards. Sometimes we get caught up in presenting a
fashionable appearance to the exclusion of more important
values. The words from 1 Peter 3:3 (GNB) apply a corrective
to such thinking: "You should not use outward aids to make
yourselves beautiful, such as the way you fix your hair, or
the jewelry you put on, or the dresses you wear. Instead,
your beauty should consist of your true inner self, the ageless beauty of a gentle and quiet spirit, which is of the
greatest value in God's sight."

In selecting furnishings and other accoutrements for
daily living, we can concentrate on utility and quality without sacrificing beauty. An example of how all these elements can be found in items of everyday furniture is seen
in "the peculiar grace of a Shaker chair which is due to the
fact that it was made by someone capable of believing that
an angel might come and sit on it."[7] Richard Nalley points
out that Shaker furniture has a utilitarian simplicity. In
the view of Shakers, the craving to be fashionable "was
foolish, a case of misplaced priorities and a waste of precious
time."[8]

Walker Percy asks a puzzling question about the state of
unhappiness observable in modern man who lives in unpar-
alleled affluence:

> Why is the good life which men have achieved in the

twentieth century so bad that only news of catastrophes, assassinations, plane crashes, mass murders, can divert one from the sadness of ordinary mornings?[9]

Perhaps Percy overdramatizes to make his point, but the fact remains that most people today rush pell-mell toward acquiring more and more things.

In a recent class assignment to university freshmen, there was nearly universal expression that money is essential for happiness. Such attitudes are so widespread that no one seems to challenge the presuppositions.

Attitudes toward wealth and its power must be scrutinized. The Bible is often misquoted to read, "Money is the root of all evil." The passage actually reads, "For the love of money is a source of all kinds of evil" (1 Tim. 6:10, GNB). The emphasis here is on attitude and relationship: The *love* of money is the cause of all kinds of evil.

The complexity of life is increased by the place of money and the love for money in the scheme of things.

There are many advantages for adopting simple tastes. For example, if we make a determined effort to save money on food, we will not only spend less but will eat better. To give careful thought to making the food dollar go farther, the shopper will give attention to good nutritional value for the money spent. Empty calories of high fat and much salt cost more than simpler and more nutritious foods.

Christians need to consider ways to economize which will conserve resources, improve the quality of life, and free us from unwanted burdens. We need to look for ways to economize in transportation, health care, energy use, household gadgets, and leisure activities, to name a few. Some careful discussion among family members and in Sunday School classes and other church units will cause persons to come up with creative and effective ways to achieve these ends.

These measures will serve as an antidote to the covetousness which dogs our steps. The Bible has much to say on this topic.

The sin of covetousness is equated with idolatry in Colossians 3:5. "Greed is a form of idolatry" (GNB). This idolatry relates to the command in Exodus 20:17, "Do not desire another man's house" (GNB). Paul summed up our duties to one another by quoting from the Ten Commandments: " 'Do not commit adultery; do not commit murder; do not steal; do not desire what belongs to someone else'—all these, and any others besides, are summed up in the one command, 'Love your neighbor as you love yourself.' If you love someone, you will never do him wrong; to love then, is to obey the whole Law' " (Rom. 13:9-10, GNB).

In the same vein, the writer of Hebrews is very explicit: "Keep your lives free from the love of money, and be satisfied with what you have. For God has said, 'I will never leave you: I will never abandon you' " (Heb. 13:5, GNB).

Jesus spoke very plainly about covetousness or greed. He classified greed with the things which make a person unclean. "It is what comes out of a person that makes him unclean. For from the inside, from a person's heart, come the evil ideas which lead him to do immoral things, to rob, kill, commit adultery, be greedy, and do all sorts of evil things; deceit, indecency, jealousy, slander, pride, and folly —all these evil things come from inside a person and make him unclean" (Mark 7:20-23, GNB).

Here are some reasons for the Christian to learn to spend less, to have less:

1. To avoid the sin of covetousness (greed).

2. To avoid the sin of idolatry.

3. To have funds to share with others.

4. To have energies to apply to other tasks.

5. To maintain a proper attitude toward material wealth.

6. To better conserve the resources of the earth.

On the other hand, there are several reasons for the Christian to earn as much as possible:

1. To have more to share.

2. To create jobs.

3. To provide for oneself and family.

4. To have power to use for betterment of community.

5. To have funds for support of the church.

It is well to keep in mind the dangers for the Christian in *desiring* wealth:

1. Sin of covetousness and greed.

2. Sin of idolatry.

3. Selfishness, self-centeredness.

4. Disregard for welfare of others.

5. Disregard for the environment and for conservation of the world's resources.

There are potential dangers for the Christian in *possessing* wealth:

1. Depending on wealth and self, not on God.

2. Feeling of being better than others.

One writer urges that we deliberately adopt a lower standard of living: "A standard of living lower in cash terms though higher in human satisfaction"[10] is a viable goal. He further asserts, "We need a thoughtful, convinced minority that will *live* in such a way as to challenge the cherished beliefs of the consumer society and defy its compulsions."[11] One stumbling block is the influence of advertising on our choices. Taylor observes, "Advertising helps enormously to create the consumer mood. It keeps things, and the value of getting things, continually before the public's eye."[12]

Advertising influences the masses to such a great degree for a variety of reasons, but one of the foremost of these is the longing to be different. Taylor observes that much of advertising "appeals to the pathetic longing of individuals to steal the march on their fellows and assert a recognizable identity so as not to be submerged in the faceless competitive tide."[13]

There are some specific actions to take regarding money, since the Bible sets forth principles and attitudes about money:

Have a plan with goals for use of money.

Save for emergencies.

Save for money to give away.

Study about insurance, savings, investments, budgets —be knowledgeable.

Read up on economics; know how economic policies affect other human beings.

Think about conservation, recycling, repairing, doing with less.

Consider simpler ways to celebrate, to give gifts.

In the general area of economics, the complexity of living can be altered, at least to a degree. The general thrust of American life is toward more and more consumption of goods and services. Action is needed to counter this trend. Many persons ask in some alarm, "If large numbers of people consume less and spend less, won't this bring on economic depression?"

This fear does not appear to have basis in fact. Educated consumers buy better quality goods as well as purchasing less. If producing better does anything, it will improve the quality of life. Savings can be re-invested to create more jobs. If Christians consume less and have more disposable incomes, more can be given away. These gifts can be channeled through the church to needy individuals and to worthwhile agencies and organizations.

A wise person will provide for emergencies, retirement, and personal responsibilities. To keep these areas in a proper balance takes thought and effort. There is an almost irresistible force in an economic system such as ours to spend, spend, spend. Intelligent consumerism provides an effective counterforce. This kind of consumerism should have strong and worthy appeal to the thoughtful Christian who seeks ways to live more simply and more sanely.

Peace and contentment do not spring from possessions and wealth. Christians have to discipline tastes and desires to make living style consonant with the biblical principle of simplicity—that life does not consist of possessions. We can emulate the examples of the saints of every age who put living the godly life ahead of affluence. To follow in their steps and, even more obediently, to follow Christ's commands will cause us all to move toward some degree of simple living.

# Notes

1. Edward A. Grubbs, *Social Aspects of the Quaker Faith* (London: Headly Brothers, 1899), p. 136.

2. Ibid, p. 137.

3. Ibid, p. 138.

4. Richard A. Easterlin, "Does Money Buy Happiness?" *Economics: A Reader*. Ed. Kenneth G. Elzinga (New York: Harper and Row, 1975), p. 113.

5. Ibid.

6. Ibid, p. 114.

7. Richard V. Nalley, "The Simple Shaker Style," *US AIR* (June 1983), p. 43.

8. Ibid.

9. Walker Percy, *The Message in a Bottle* (New York: Farrar, Straus, and Giroux, 1980), p. 7.

10. John V. Taylor, *Enough Is Enough* (Minneapolis: Augsburg Publishing House, 1977), p. 63.

11. Ibid, p. 65.

12. Ibid, p. 66.

13. Ibid, p. 67.

# 5

# THE SEARCH FOR ENOUGH TIME

## Necessity and Challenge

Time present and time past
Are both perhaps present in time future,
And time future contained in time past.
If all time is eternally present
All time is redeemable.

—T. S. Eliot[1]

The Bible admonishes us to redeem the time because the days are evil. To make such redemption is both a challenge and a necessity for the believer who wishes to simplify and to make effective use of the time allotted. To simplify our use of time and the ways we allocate our days and hours, there are many things to keep in mind. Even though the years of our lifespan are unknown to us, we each have the same number of hours in the day we are living. We see many friends and colleagues who seem to do more in the same amount of time than others and who at the same time seem less hurried and in better control of their time.

The question arises, how do they do it? What can I do to achieve a more simplified approach and have more control

55

of the days and hours of my life? The Bible speaks to this issue in specific terms. The writer of Ecclesiastes asserts, "Everything that happens in this world happens at the time God chooses" (Eccl. 3:1, GNB).

But what is the concept, *time,* of which we speak so glibly? A look at the dictionary gives an intriguing definition: Time is "all the days there have ever been or ever will be; the past, present, and future."[2] Another dictionary defines time as "A nonspatial continuum in which events occur in apparently irreversible succession from past through the present to the future."[3]

From these concepts of the over-arching reach of time in the framework of the human mind, we need to focus on the days, the continuum from past to present, which is ours to use and to enjoy.

One thinks of the dictum of the literary world in the late nineteenth century, *carpe diem,* seize the day! This brings to mind the words of Jesus to his disciples, "So do not worry about tomorrow; it will have enough worries of its own. There is no need to add to the troubles each day brings" (Matt. 6:34, GNB). In a more earthbound context, the poet says, "But at my back I always hear/Time's winged chariot hurrying near."[4]

For those who feel threatened by the speed at which most of our lives are lived, there is comfort in the words from Ecclesiastes 9:11-12: "In this world fast runners do not always win the races, and the brave do not always win the battles. Wise men do not always earn a living, intelligent men do not always get rich, and capable men do not always rise to high positions. Bad luck happens to everyone. You never know when your time is coming" (GNB).

The apostle Paul described the duties of believers to obey the commandments and to love one another. Then he said, "You must do this, because you know that the time has come for you to wake up from your sleep" (Rom. 13:11, GNB). This message is motivation for action, for planning, and for proper use of time.

Hosea gave the direction of the Lord which sets forth activities for the use of time: "Plow new ground for yourselves, plant righteousness, and reap the blessings that your devotion to me will produce. It is time for you to turn to me, your Lord, and I will come and pour out blessings upon you" (Hos. 10:12, GNB).

James in his epistle to the church added a sense of urgency with his words, "You don't even know what your life tomorrow will be! You are like a puff of smoke, which appears for a moment and then disappears. What you should say is this: 'If the Lord is willing, we will live and do this or that' " (Jas. 4:14-15, GNB).

In Sonnet LX Shakespeare spoke of the passage of time. He described the marks that time inflicts on all humans:

> Like as the waves make towards the pebbled shore,
> So do our minutes hasten to their end;
> Each changing place with that which goes before
> In sequent toil all forwards to contend.
> Nativity, once in the main of light,
> Crawls to maturity, wherewith being crowned,
> Crooked eclipses 'gainst his glory fight,
> And Time that gave doth now his gift confound.
> Time doth transfix the flourish set on youth,
> And delves the parallels in beauty's brow,
> Feeds on the rarities of nature's truth,
> And nothing stands but for his scythe to mow.

And yet to times in hope my verse shall stand,
Praising worth, despite his cruel hand.[5]

With all these admonitions and observations before us,
we should remember that "there are qualitative differences
between time measured and time lived."[6]

It is imperative that each of us decides on our own needs
and priorities and then includes time for self, family,
friends, prayer and meditation, personal interests, and personal growth. In order to achieve these priorities, we must
examine the many ways available to us to go about simplifying our use of time. Planning ahead and using a calendar
are tried and true techniques. Such planning gives an over-
view of where time is spent and allows some control in time
allocation. We need to learn to say no to avoid letting others
set our priorities and allocate our time.

In this connection, Elton Trueblood has written:

> Most people whom I know are too busy. It is a common
> experience to see people rushing in every direction, no
> one having time to contemplate or to speak slowly with
> friends. At worst, we become a hectic generation, always
> running to keep up or to maintain overdemanding
> schedules. We have many luxuries, we ride in fine cars,
> and we live in beautifully furnished homes, but what we
> do not have, in our civilization, is time to appreciate. The
> fact that nearly all people in our particular culture are
> too busy is, indeed, a paradox. We have invented and
> produced numerous labor saving devices, which might
> reasonably be expected to provide us with time, but some-
> how this expected consequence does not occur. We ought
> to have the time used by our ancestors to bring the water
> from the spring, to chop the firewood, to trim the lamp
> wick, to weave the cloth and so much more, but strangely

the freedom purchased by mechanical skill appears to be lost.[7]

Trueblood believes this loss is the result in part from overscheduling, from underestimating time required for tasks, and from attempting to do too many things each day. "Life would be far better for all concerned if each person tried to do fewer things, with a chance to finish each before starting another, thereby achieving some peace of mind."[8]

One key is in the term "peace of mind." Most people in today's culture are desperately aware of the lack of peace in their innermost being but seem to have no clear idea of how to find the calm and comfort that comes from inner peace. Prayer, contemplation, and meditation are at best unused if not unknown disciplines for Christians.

We need to learn how to pray, how to be contemplative, how to use periods of meditation, and how to profitably study the Bible and books about the Bible and the Christian life.

One professional counselor with a full and busy life is an example of knowing how to say no and to retain control of her own time. When asked to do one more task, serve on one more committee, or attend a luncheon, she will examine her calendar, make up her mind, then respond with a firm but pleasant, "No, I am so sorry, but I cannot do that." She does not spend needless time in explaining and justifying her decision. Her refusal is accepted without question, her relationship to the inviter is not harmed, and she has remained in control of her own life.

Many times we are timid, fearful, and overestimate our own importance when we take on tasks we do not have time or interest in doing. With careful discipline and consistent practice, we can do as this counselor does and politely but firmly say, "No, I am sorry, but I cannot do that." The earth won't spin out of orbit, and good work will go on. We can then make our work more pleasant and the results of higher quality.

Perhaps for those who have a tendency to overschedule, a regularly monthly or quarterly session with their calendar and a list of priorities and goals to re-evaluate planning, performance, and preference will aid in taking charge and assuring a simpler approach to daily living. One should ask, "Whose life is it anyway?" and remember that the spending of time is the spending of life. To spend it wisely is to be good stewards of the gifts God has given. To develop the gift of simplicity is to develop a plan and a style of using the hours of each day in a manner both simple and fruitful and satisfying.

Dru Scott, writing about personal time management, observes:

> Our capacity for accomplishments, recreation, and relationships grows from a strong sense of our personal value, our being. No amount of work and no accomplishment can confirm or challenge our being, because being does not depend on doing. Doing can lead to satisfaction and the sense of accomplishment, but it will never substitute for the realization of your own personal worth. Affirm your value as a multifaceted individual. Enjoy a rich variety of time investments. Open yourself to the joys of this moment whether they are in recreation, relationships, or work accomplishments.[9]

To resolve the tensions inherent in planning and scheduling one's time versus the need to be unhurried and to have the freedom to be spontaneous takes careful and thoughtful attention. It is a struggle that is never ending—a battle that has its lulls but that goes on as long as a person is actively involved in purposeful living. To live in some style of simplicity requires a courageous and constant effort to keep the freedom and yet plan properly to get tasks done and see goals reached. Stated another way, this facet of simple living is a matter of attitude. To work at viewing life as a balance between commitment to plans and calendars and openness to spontaneity and time for contemplation is a matter of reassuring oneself that it is all right. It is a proper, good, and appropriate use of time. Time can be redeemed in quietness and in joy as well as in activity and in duty.

To achieve everyday success in getting more time into one's life, Dru Scott suggests that central and essential activities be done first. Grouping related activities together is another way to save time. By one's dividing big tasks into workable small units, the work becomes possible. Such subdividing makes the work within reach rather than overwhelming. Using a timetable to keep on track also helps. Concentrating on doing only one thing at a time will ensure steady achievement. Finishing the task at hand and doing the task *now* are two other methods for getting things done that one can incorporate into daily habits.[10]

It is essential to clarify to yourself what is of highest value in your scheme of things. Setting goals and establishing priorities are aids to using time to advantage. It is easy to slip into allowing others to decide for you what should take up your time and energy. Courage and determination must be exercised in order to stay with what *you* think is worth your time and effort.

Psychologists have written many books and articles to

teach the reader how to motivate and reward actions in order to reach goals. Understanding some of these principles will prove helpful in getting done the things that are important to you.

Jesus reminded us to concentrate on today and not worry about tomorrow. If we follow his admonitions as well as using the best that modern psychologists can tell us, we will enhance the quality and the use of time. Better use and more careful allocation will result in more contentment, greater peace, and simpler living.

Some practical ways to take charge of one's time can include some of the following actions. When you see that you must wait in line, decide to enjoy the wait. Determine not to be upset and not to have an impatient attitude. Use the time to reflect, to watch the scene around you, to dream, to plan. These are positive and productive actions. When pressured to get to an appointment in a short time only to be held up by heavy traffic, take charge of your attitude. Use the enforced wait to pray, to reflect, to enjoy being alive.

Perhaps these actions and attitudes which reflect patience and acceptance are another way of saying, "Take charge of what can be changed and change it. Accept what cannot be changed without fretting and worrying." This kind of taking oneself in hand can be done with determination and practice. It is well worth the effort and the time it takes. One result will be a feeling of making decisions about your life rather than being put upon by events and by other people. The quietness of spirit and the calm attitude which result will enrich life for you and for those around you. It is worth a try!

# Notes

1. T. S. Eliot, "Burnt Norton," *The Four Quartets* (New York: Harcourt, Brace and World, 1943), p. 13.

2. *Thorndike Barnhart Comprehensive Desk Dictionary* (Garden City: Doubleday, 1969).

3. *The American Heritage Dictionary of the English Language*. Ed. William Morris (Boston: American Heritage Publishing Co., 1969).

4. Andrew Marvell, "To His Coy Mistress," *The Poem: an Anthology*. Ed. Stanley B. Green and A. Kingsley Weatherhead (New York: Appleton-Century-Crofts, 1968), p. 102.

5. William Shakespeare, "Sonnet LX," *Shakespeare's Sonnets*. Ed. Hyder E. Rollins (New York: Appleton-Century-Crofts, 1951), p. 30.

6. Lawrence LeShan and Henry Margenau, *Einstein's Space and Van Gogh's Sky* (New York: Macmillan Company, 1982), p. 157.

7. Elton Trueblood, *Quarterly Yoke Letter*, vol. 22 (Dec. 1980), no. 4, p. 1.

8. Ibid.

9. Dru Scott, *How to Put More Time Into Your Life* (New York: Rawson Wade Publishers, 1980), p. 197.

10. Ibid, p. 104.

# 6

# THE SEARCH FOR SERENITY

## Emotions and Relationships

How can emotions make life more complex? Emotions use up energy; feelings affect the ways we allocate our time and attention. Since we are both rational and irrational creatures, the way we feel is just as important as the way we think. Feelings have great potential for determining how successful a person is in developing a simple life-style and being content with this manner of living. To live simply and to be free, we need to know how to deal with feelings about ourselves, our lives, and our relationships with the important other persons in our lives.

A physician has said, "Feelings without honesty are defenses. The world without honesty is an illusion. Memory without honesty is only a fantasy. Time without honesty can never be now. Space without honesty can never be here. Love without honesty is possessiveness."[1]

In looking at emotions and relationships, one must first consider the relationship to God. Then attention can be directed toward feelings toward self, toward others, and then to the underlying feelings in all three relationships.

First, and most important, is the relationship with God.

Jesus said that the first and greatest commandment is to love God with all our hearts and minds. He continued by saying that the second commandment is equally important: to love our neighbor as we love ourselves. In his teachings Jesus emphasized that we must put the kingdom of God first, letting all other things fall in place after this highest priority. To live in right relationship with God, loving him with our hearts and minds, is no easy matter. This takes prayer, dedication, discipline, study, effort, and communion with him.

Second, we need a proper view of self. To love our neighbor as ourselves means we must love ourselves. There is a rash of popular books addressing the need for proper self-esteem. These volumes emphasize that one must have a healthy and positive value of self in order to love and to value others. M. Scott Peck defines love in a way that applies here: "Love . . . is the will to extend one's self for the purpose of nurturing one's own or another's spiritual growth."[2] Coming from another angle but with pertinent ideas, David Burns asserts that persons should not base the opinion of self on achievements. He believes that "self-worth based on accomplishments is 'pseudo-esteem,' not the genuine thing. You cannot base your self-worth on looks, talent, fame or fortune." He insists that love and approval cannot add to a human being's inherent worth. Burns says that a person's sense of self-worth determines how one *feels*.[3]

Third, people need good relations with the most important persons in their lives. These significant persons include spouse, children, parents, extended family members, fellow Christians, and colleagues. With these relationships in good order, we will be free to take on our share of responsibility for all persons everywhere. We are responsible to pray for and to care for all persons since God is Creator of all humankind.

Fourth, friendships are extremely important; friends are vital to a life of contentment and simplicity. We benefit from having someone who cares for us, listens to us, and accepts us as we are. In this connection C. S. Lewis has defined friendship in a meaningful and interesting way:

> Notice that Friendship thus repeats on a more individual and less socially necessary level the character of the Companionship which was its matrix. The Companionship was between two people who were doing something together, but something more or less inward, less widely shared, and less easily defined; still hunters, but of some immaterial quarry; still collaborating, but in some work the world does not, or not yet, take account of; still traveling companions, but on a different kind of journey. Hence we picture lovers face to face but Friends side by side; their eyes look ahead.[4]

In an effort and plan to move toward simplicity, attention must be given to dealing with one's own feelings and in maintaining good relationships with others. To achieve these goals, there are some do's and don't's to keep in mind. First, don't try to control the lives of others. This is important and difficult in dealing with those who are most important to us. It is well to keep in mind how responsible you would feel if someone did what you advised, and the action taken had disastrous results. An extreme example is to urge someone to marry only to have the marriage fail, or to advise a job change and the job plays out or the person cannot perform successfully. The blame comes back quickly to you: "You told me to do this. Now look at the mess I'm in."

To listen sympathetically, to help see options and possible results, to think through situations—these are helpful actions. To help is far from controlling. Helpful but not controlling actions will keep relationships less complicated, more simple, and more lasting.

Another action to take is to avoid being dependent on other people for your happiness, contentment, and purpose in life. Others should not determine your activities and commitments. How often we hear others and even hear our own complaining voices say, "If only you (or he or she) had done (or not done) thus and so, then I would be better off." Too often we say or think, "If this person would do this, then I would be so happy." To place our lives and our happiness in the hands of anyone other than the Lord is to abdicate personal responsibility and to sink into a complicating dependent role.

If we allow ourselves to establish patterns of dependency, we create traps for those dear to us. We make escape hatches to explain away our own false steps. It is only by accepting full responsibility for ourselves that we grow and that we shape our hearts and minds more in the mold of our model, Jesus of Nazareth.

It is essential that we do not look to others to reflect self-respect and self-confidence. Such flattery may be most pleasant on the occasions when it happens, but to rely on finding self-respect in the mirror of the eyes of others is a dangerous path to take. To learn to have good self-concept and self-respect, to be brave enough to know where we stand, is to become more self-reliant and to shed shackles that complicate life. This course of action takes courage and determination since we almost always watch others to see how we are doing. It is a human reaction to gauge the expressions of approval or disapproval in the faces of our companions and to adjust actions accordingly. We yearn for approval and acceptance.

It is a paradox that the more one tailors conduct to win approval, the less approval will be forthcoming. As noted in the lives of heroes and in accounts of courageous actions, it is often necessary to act alone. To achieve integrity, one must be willing to speak out against prevailing opinions. Sometimes to be true to ideals and convictions, it is necessary to walk alone. These brave deeds arise from persons who have a good self-regard and who have respect for themselves.

It took courage for Carl to pursue his call to Christian ministry. He had to make his preparation and plans in the face of opposition from family and friends. Those who loved him felt he ought to use his talents in a profession that would have prestige, high income, and opportunities for career advancement that did not seem possible in church-related work. To go alone against these persons required Carl's being certain of his own judgment and brave enough to act alone.

Among some do's for more simplicity and contentment in the sphere of emotions and relationships is the advice to practice desired attitudes and behavior patterns. For example, practice self-reliance. It may work best to begin in small acts. Resist the temptation to fall back on others when you can take care of matters yourself. Learn to depend first and foremost on God. We know that he is always available. He has promised to never leave us or forsake us.

Express appreciation. Tell people you care for them. Say,

"I love you," to those whom you truly love. Even though they know you love them, say it.

Learn to give constructive criticism. This kind of help is meaningful to you and your friends. Learn to make self-criticism constructive. This means seeing in faults and failures the good things, the positive aspects, and then building a course of action to expand on the good.

Accept your strong feelings and learn ways to use this reservoir of energy for good purposes. One woman finds that the best outlet for her anger is to clean closets. Another person will find relief in competitive sports. Janie has been advised by her physician to take an hour's walk when she is overcome by anger, fear, or anxiety. Each person can find acceptable and workable ways to harness strong feelings which could be destructive to make them work for good ends, for constructive purposes.

It is possible that these arguments may sound too much like blatant disregard for others. These proposals are not meant to suggest being heedless of the feelings and opinions of other people. There are occasions when we cannot avoid altering our desires to take into account the well-being of others. The bottom line of these suggestions is that a person must be a whole, well-integrated, and self-respecting person in order to be able to work in concert with others. It is something of a restatement of the wisdom in Jesus' command to love others as one loves oneself.

There is a healthy tension in love for others and love for self. Such a balancing of tensions can result in a reconciliation between self-reliance, reliance on God, and approval from others. Opinions and encouragement are important to every human being. We truly need the good opinion of others. We can develop our own gift for simple living and pursue life in a simplified manner when we find the middle ground and are able to depend on God and ourselves. It takes courage to stand alone against the mainstream, but the mature Christian will search for the place to stand whether it provides companions or not.

Since Christians often have difficulty in dealing with strong negative emotions, it is worthwhile to give some thought to how to deal with fear, anger, anxiety, and guilt in order to free up time and energy. Each of us can come up with a list of actions and attitudes for those times when we are overwhelmed by our own strong feelings. Some ways which might be explored include:

Admit that you are feeling anger, fear, guilt.

Express these feelings in some positive manner.

Learn how to forgive yourself.

Remember that God forgives. Ask him.

Learn ways to redirect your thoughts to more positive areas.

Make a plan of action to correct or change what can be corrected or changed.

Take action on some part of the plan, regardless of how small or insignificant the action may seem.

Deliberately take a hard look at the situation and get things into proportion.

Remember Jesus' admonition that we are to forgive seventy times seven. This means forgiving others and forgiving self. Christians need to be mindful of the word of God that vengeance belongs to him. Review the plan of action for the Christian which Paul described in Romans 12. Then you can find the truth of his command: "Do not let evil defeat you; instead, conquer evil with good" (Rom. 12:21, GNB).

The Bible speaks to the believer when oppressed by worry

and anxiety: "Don't worry about anything, but in all your prayers ask God for what you need, always asking him with a thankful heart. And God's peace, which is far beyond human understanding, will keep your hearts and minds safe in union with Christ Jesus" (Phil. 4:6, GNB).

A helpful passage for dealing with impatience is found in the words of the psalmist: "Be patient and wait for the Lord to act;/don't be worried about those who prosper/or those who succeed in their evil plans./Don't give in to worry or anger;/it only leads to trouble" (Ps. 37:7-8, GNB).

Anger can be abated by prayerful reading of James 1:19-21, GNB: "Remember this, my dear brothers! Everyone must be quick to listen, but slow to speak and slow to become angry. Man's anger does not achieve God's righteous purpose. So get rid of every filthy habit and all wicked conduct. Submit to God and accept the word that he plants in your hearts, which is able to save you."

Reread and contemplate the positive emotions and attitudes described by Paul as fruits of the spirit in Galatians 5:22.

The Bible, both Old Testament and New Testament, encourages families to exist in love, harmony, and unity. Parents are to be respected. Children are to obey their parents and accept parental discipline, but parents are urged to avoid provoking anger in the child. Families in the Bible demonstrate caring for the ill and the aged, extending forgiveness (Joseph and his brothers, the prodigal son), and giving attention to the things of God (Mary and Martha).

Relationships with families and friends are potential sources of great joy and deep sadness. By our practicing Christian virtues and employing the teachings from the Bible, life can be more satisfying, less complicated, more content, and less frustrating. Energy can be directed to productive ends. We will be well on the way of developing the gift of simplicity in our relationship to God, to ourselves, and to those with whom we live.

# Notes

1. David Viscott, *The Language of Feelings* (New York: Pocket Books, 1976), pp. 147-48.

2. M. Scott Peck, *The Road Less Traveled* (New York: Simon & Schuster, 1978), p. 81.

3. David Burns, *Feeling Good: The New Mood Therapy* (New York: William Morrow, 1980), quoted in "Think Your Way Out of Depression," *Reader's Digest* (Dec. 1980), p. 127.

4. C. S. Lewis, *The Joyful Christian* (New York: Macmillan Co., 1977), p. 192.

# 7

# THE SEARCH FOR WELL-BEING
## Complications of Modern Stress

Among the distinctive characteristics of modern American life is the prevalence of stress in all aspects of our culture and society. The June 6, 1983 issue of *Time* magazine devoted its cover story to this growing affliction. The editors of *Time* noted that "no one really knows if there is more stress now than in the past, but many experts believe it has become more pervasive."[1]

Even though we would be hard pressed to define in exact scientific terms just what stress is and how it affects the body, we are aware of its presence in daily living. Almost everyone has experienced the headaches, the fatigue, and the indigestion which is ascribed to stress, to pressure, to the feeling of not being in control. Many see a connection between the effects of stressful conditions and the breakdown in family life. Some connect cancer, heart disease, and hypertension to stress. Many have experienced depression and other emotional upsets that seem to be related to the stressful environment in which we exist.

In the face of our affluent manner of living, it is a mystery that so many are incapacitated to varying degrees by the stresses they experience. In more primitive cultures and in less affluent circumstances, so much time and effort are spent on acquiring the basics that apparently little room is left for energy or attention to be caught up in activities that seem to result in destructive stress symptoms.

The story is told that in England during World War II the number of patients in mental hospitals drastically declined. The country was geared up to resist the bombings of the Nazi forces and the people were preparing to follow Churchill's declaration to fight to the very doorsteps. Why would such a dangerous situation—certainly one causing wear and tear on the body and the mind—why would such a stressful situation relieve the normal load of emotional distress in the population? A puzzle. A solution could give clues for handling the stresses which overwhelm us and make so many experience the misery and pain of depression and despair.

Today's conversations are filled with remarks about too much pressure, burnout, stress response, and psychosomatic illnesses. Physicians and researchers investigate the emotional causes of every kind of disease from cancer to arthritis. Hardly any issue of the daily paper or popular magazines is without an article related to the effects of stress on some aspect of life, whether it is physical, emotional, relational, or spiritual.

There are some who believe that the disconnection from the cycles of nature has interfered with the healthy functioning of the whole person. One example that comes to mind is the process of tanning of the skin. In ancient days when most people lived on the land and engaged in raising of crops, gradual exposure to the sun began in early spring. The tanning process proceeded gradually so that by midsummer the skin was protected from the damaging rays of the more intense sunlight.

Today people living in cities rush the process of getting that tanned, healthy, outdoor look. In the rush, the skin is ravaged by too fast and too intense exposure to damaging rays. The intent is no longer protection while out in the sunlight working but a browned skin for appearance's sake entirely.

This change in behavior illustrates a good many aspects of how the move away from the close identification with the rhythms of the seasons has complicated the way we live. The stress talked about and widely experienced does seem to be a phenomena of modern industrialized society.

Dr. Hans Selye, a Canadian researcher, was the pioneer of studies into the causes and results of stress and distress. Dr. Selye defines stress as "the non-specific response of the body to any demand made upon it."[2] He notes that a specific demand occurs when the body is exposed to cold, causing shivers which produce more heat. All specific demands create specific actions and also increase the demand for readjustment. "This demand is nonspecific; it requires adaptation to a problem, irrespective of what the problem may be."[3] "From the point of view of its stress-producing or stressor activity, it is immaterial whether the agent or situation we face is pleasant or unpleasant; all that counts is the intensity of the demand for readjustment of adaption."[4] Selye asserts that "the stress is not merely nervous tension; it is not something to be avoided; it is not the result of normal, intense but pleasant activity; and it is not complete freedom from stress."[5] Complete freedom from stress is death!

For those persons dealing with modern stress, there are

many possible causes of the destructive effects. Among these suspected culprits are the frantic pace of everyday life, the uncertainties of daily living, and the shadows on the future. Other causes are the upheavals in modern government, politics, and economics, the radical changes in the basic values of life, and the rapid changes in the roles of men and women. The lack of a generally accepted standard of conduct in human relationships and the increasing de-emphasis of the mystery, the spiritual, and the irrational in this scientific age make for stress also.

According to the Academy of Family Physicians, as reported in *Time* magazine, "Two-thirds of office visits to family doctors are prompted by stress-related symptoms."[6]

The writer of the *Time* article insists that "Our mode of life itself, the way we live, is emerging as today's principal cause of illness."[7] Also, Type A personalities are cited as being persons who suffer from the damaging effects of stress. These people have "the tendency to try to accomplish too many things in too little time . . . there is free-floating hostility. These people are irritated by trivial things; they exhibit signs of struggle against time and other people."[8]

Dr. Selye discriminates between normal, necessary stress and the damaging stressors. He says:

> Mental tensions, frustrations, insecurity, and aimlessness are among the most damaging stressors, and psychosomatic studies have shown how often they cause migraine headaches, peptic ulcers, heart attacks, hypertension, mental disease, suicide, or just hopeless unhappiness.[9]

Summing up the positive and negative aspects of stress, Dr. Selye observes:

In interpersonal stress, the gain is incitement in others of friendship, gratitude, goodwill and love toward ourselves; the loss is the creation in others of hatred, frustration, and an urge for revenge. This applies both to people around us and to ourselves, for our own positive or negative feelings toward others respectively benefit or hurt us directly, just as much as we are helped or hurt by inciting those feelings in others.[10]

Here are examples of persons experiencing and coping with a variety of ordinary stresses.

Mack and Mary Ann sit side by side, gripping each other's hands as they talk with their pastor. "We adopted Mike because we wanted a child so badly. We tried to do everything right. Why has he become so rebellious? He skips school; he won't listen to us; we are at the end of our rope. What can we do?" This couple is experiencing stress as they see a young man they love committing self-destructive acts.

Bill and Barbara stare into the firelight as they sit in the midst of packing boxes, opened closets, lists of final things to do before moving. "We've had ten good years here. We shall miss this house, the neighbors, our friends." He turns toward his wife and sees her head bowed as she catches tears with the edge of her sleeve. "I know we are doing the right thing to move, but why is it so painful? Why do I grieve so?" Barbara asks. This couple is experiencing a definite stress, a life-changing event that causes both pain and joy.

Fred lives alone in a high rise building for the elderly. He is divorced and has only occasional contact with his children and grandchildren. He is moderately active in the adult class of a nearby church but has few friends. Loneliness is a chief adversary. He must also cope with declining strength and failing health. He muses, "Ah, I wonder when

I'll have my second heart attack. Who will look after me when I can't see after myself?" Loneliness and poor health. Concern for the future. Anxiety about becoming dependent. Stress-producing factors without doubt.

Janie is an active church member, a committed Christian. She teaches in the three-year-old Sunday School and sings in the choir. Coming into the house at 12:30 Sunday following church services, anger and frustration rise, filling her body with a surging tide of bitterness. The house is in disarray from the hasty dressing and departure of three hours earlier. Before she can begin lunch, the breakfast dishes must be cleared. Heroically stifling the urge to scream, she lays down her purse and Bible and methodically begins to straighten the kitchen while putting the beef in to brown for the spaghetti sauce. The meal is spread. Paul says the blessing over the salad, spaghetti, and hot French bread. After serving the baby's plate, Janie begins to eat, only to be stopped midway with a surging, pounding, excruciating headache.

In periods of high unemployment, newspapers and other periodicals are filled with studies and human interest articles describing the debilitating effects of loss of job on every kind of person. The situations and levels of real need will vary from one area of the nation to another. Persons facing the harsh realities of little or no income react with varying degrees of hopelessness and ingenious efforts to find alternative ways to exist. Several overriding factors seem to afflict every unemployed person at some point: depression, feelings of uselessness, and despair.

Dan has completed college and seminary. He is trained, eager to meet human need, ready to get started in ministry. His applying to denominational agencies has not produced even an interview. Churches want a pastor with experience. How does an able, called young man support himself and enter into his vocation without the invitation of some church or some group? No wonder Dan has to struggle with despair and with questions about his place in God's plan.

Mike is a young but qualified construction worker. He has faithfully completed the requirements of his union to prove his capabilities and has several months of on-the-job experience. He can do the work. Suddenly the home-building market slumps; there is no work at all. Eventually the unemployment benefits are used up. Mike has to look in his mirror to see a strong, qualified, and willing worker who can find no one who will hire him. His self-esteem drops; he begins to experience aches and pains in his body as well as the questioning and self-doubt that harrows his mind and spirit. Unemployment causes all manner of stress and elicits multiple distress symptoms.

Stress complicates our lives in many ways. A society oriented so totally toward consuming as ours breeds stress just as it seems to breed violence. In a call to simpler living, there is a plea for people to move to living on a lower level in terms of cash expended and goods consumed. There is a call to peace. This call to simplicity will result in a higher level of satisfaction in direct proportion to the lowering of consuming and getting and possessing.

We need a radical change in attitudes in order to change and to lower the devastating levels of stress in our lives. To study the Bible is good and desirable, but we must give attention to its teachings in such ways that apply to our actual behavior. We have truly learned the truths of Scripture only when we change what we do, what we say, how we feel toward others, and how we treat others.

A principle for coping with stress and lowering stress levels is clearly stated in the wise advice to avoid excess. The ancient ideal of the Golden Mean can be considered and applied to our living. Also, the New Testament teachings on temperance can be examined and applied.

In the face of all the multiple causes of stress, distress, and the resulting handicapping effects, most experts point out that the stress-causing *events* are not the most important, but the *attitudes* one has and how one deals with stress are the keys to coping.

Psychologists point to several personal factors that appear to be helpful, "among them: the sense of being in control of one's life, having a network of friends or family to provide what researchers call 'social support,' and such personality factors as flexibility and hopefulness."[11]

There are many reasons to learn to cope with stress:

—To combat the frantic pace of everyday life.
—To cope with the uncertainties of modern life.
—To live with the upheavals in modern government, politics, and the economy.
—To live with the radical changes in basic values.
—To cope with the rapid changes in the roles of men and women.
—To cope with the lack of standard of conduct in relationships.
—To combat the de-emphasis of the mystery, the spiritual, the irrational in this scientific age.

Dr. Selye believes that to cope with stress a person needs to take action when the task is too difficult. Then stop. Then change activity. He insists that one not rest or become merely inactive. After stopping and changing, resume the task. The principle is that to deal with stress on the brain, a person needs to change to muscle stress. "Stress on one system helps to relax another."[12]

Selye's advice for avoiding distress is to avoid frustration; avoid humiliation and failure; avoid aiming too high. Avoid tasks too difficult to do. "Within the limits set by our innate abilities, we should strive for excellence, for the best we can do." We ought not strive for perfection which is unattainable; such goals lead to distress and frustration.[13]

Also, Christians can keep in mind scriptural admonitions to be still, take no thought for tomorrow, be content with what you have, and trust in the Lord. These actions can lead to less stress and greater simplicity.

# How Vulnerable Are You to Stress?

The following test was developed by psychologists Lyle H. Miller and Alma Dell Smith at Boston University Medical Center and published in *Time* (June 6, 1983), p. 54. Score each item from 1 (almost always) to 5 (never), according to how much of the time each statement applies to you.

\_\_1.  I eat at least one hot, balanced meal a day.

\_\_2.  I get seven to eight hours sleep at least four nights a week.

\_\_3.  I give and receive affection regularly.

\_\_4.  I have at least one relative within fifty miles on whom I can rely.

\_\_5.  I exercise to the point of perspiration at least twice a week.

\_\_6.  I smoke less than half a pack of cigarettes a day.

\_\_7.  I take fewer than five alcoholic drinks a week.

\_\_8.  I am the appropriate weight for my height.

\_\_9.  I have an income adequate to meet basic expenses.

\_\_10. I get strength from my religious beliefs.

\_\_11. I regularly attend club or social activities.

\_\_12. I have a network of friends and acquaintances.

\_\_13. I have one or more friends to confide in about personal matters.

\_\_14. I am in good health (including eyesight, hearing, teeth).

\_\_15. I am able to speak openly about my feelings when angry or worried.

\_\_16. I have regular conversations with the people I live with about domestic problems, e.g., chores, money, and daily living issues.

\_\_17. I do something for fun at least once a week.

\_\_18. I am able to organize my time effectively.

\_\_19. I drink fewer than three cups of coffee (or tea or cola drinks) a day.

\_\_20. I take quiet time for myself during the day.

To get your score, add up the figures and subtract twenty. Any number over thirty indicates a vulnerability to stress. You are seriously vulnerable if your score is between fifty and seventy-five, and extremely vulnerable if it is over seventy-five.

# Notes

1. "Stress: Can We Cope?" *Time* (June 6, 1983), p. 48.

2. Hans Selye, *Stress Without Distress* (New York: J. B. Lippincott, 1974), p. 27.

3. Ibid, p. 28.

4. Ibid, p. 29.

5. Ibid, pp. 31-32.

6. *Time,* p. 48.

7. Ibid.

8. Ibid, p. 52.

9. Selye, pp. 108-109.

10. Ibid, p. 74.

11. *Time,* p. 50.

12. Selye, p. 81.

13. Ibid, p. 109.

# 8

# THE SEARCH FOR A PLACE "IN" BUT NOT "OF" THE WORLD

## Intricacies of the Culture

The young teacher sat by the lakeside, seeking rest and quiet. His efforts were of little use; a crowd soon surrounded him. People appeared in knots as though a magician had flicked a silken handkerchief and produced men and women rather than the usual brightly colored flowers. Soon the crowd pressed in so that the teacher edged toward a rowboat pulled up on the bank. He slipped onto the hard seat and rowed a few yards away. From his position in the swaying boat, he spoke to the eager faces edging the shore.

Jesus' pulling away from the crowd in order to see them and to make certain they could hear him is a lesson for Christians desiring to bear witness. To be effective and to be heard, Jesus separated himself from the crowd. So it is with Christians: To be believable and authentic there must be a difference which is readily discernible. However, the separation from the world should not be so harsh and so distant that the unconverted cannot see, hear, and be drawn to the Savior by the lives of his followers.

Being *in* the world but not *of* the world is an age-old tension. Christians and the church live in constant danger of becoming captives of the culture in which they exist. Virginia Stem Owens has observed that Christians need to analyze the aping of secular society to find a guide for determining what is fitting and proper to expressions of the Christian faith. A standard for making decisions should be something beyond the American pragmatist question, "Does it work?"[1]

The human desire for black and white answers, for a list of specific do's and don't's, makes it hard to decide what is "worldly" and what is uniquely Christian. So many values are embedded in the culture that it is difficult to make unambiguous decisions. Since culture is the way we transmit beliefs, behavior, and institutions to our children, it is imperative that we take a long look at the culture, ourselves, and our Christian beliefs.

Order, tradition, ceremony, custom—these are essential to civilized human society. W. B. Yeats spoke to this point in his poem "A Prayer for My Daughter."

> And may her bridegroom bring her to a house
> Where all's accustomed, ceremonious;
> For arrogance and hatred are the wares
> Peddled in the thoroughfares.
> How but in custom and in ceremony
> Are innocence and beauty born?[2]

Yeats underscored the point that custom and ceremony are required for a full, meaningful life.

The adults of the twentieth century have a peculiar problem in the task of transmitting cultural values to their children. Custom, ceremony, and other matters must be taught. Margaret Mead addressed the modern barrier in her discussions of the school in American culture.

"The adults in the modern world face children who are not only unlike their own past childhood, but who are actually unlike any children who have ever been in the world before." We are living in a new world because of modernization and technology. Those who were born before World War II and are living in this new world are very far removed from those born during this period. It is not unlike the move to the new world of Europeans in the early years of this country. The first generation brought what they knew from Europe, the second generation knew nothing but what they learned in the new world. Also, the present generation gap is different from any before. It is a world-wide phenomenon because of world communications. Events on the other side of the globe are ours as well. Mead said, "For the first time the young are seeing history made before it is censored by their elder." Children of the modern era know what their parents cannot know. In the past, elders had the experience of living in a culture which the children did not yet have. Now culture has changed and the adults cannot know all that our culture entails.[3]

A significant aspect of American culture which has extraordinary influence today—an aspect which is a new thing in the world—is the ascendancy of television. Debates rage and wither, then rise and fall regarding the extent of its influence on culture and whether the influence is good or bad. It seems that television and other media of communications in America do overload the minds of viewers. The population is dulled to real emotion by seeing too much that is effectually unreal. Events and scenes are presented daily which should provoke horror, revulsion, rage, pity, and fear, or happenings that ought to cause great joy and celebration. Instead, the immediacy and the artificiality of the television screen put such distance between viewer and event that genuine feelings are effectively dulled.

Malcolm Muggeridge examined the idea of Christ and the media. He stated that he became involved in "the interminable inquest as to whether it (television) can be considered a debit or credit item in our popular culture: as stimulating, or merely reflecting, the growing depravity and violence of our way of life; as a cause or a consequence of growing illiteracy; as a window on the world, or a mirror reflecting all too faithfully our world's absurdities and inanities."[4]

The power of television is dramatically described by Owens in a discussion of the assassinations of John Kennedy and Martin Luther King, Jr., in the early sixties. "Just as the assassinations would perhaps never have occurred without the promise of appearing on television, so television would never have become the final arbiter of American politics without the assassinations."[5] In an equally strong statement Muggeridge questions the veracity of television news coverage. "News is ten million people induced to think the same thing, which makes it a thousand times more false in the unlikely event of its happening to be true."[6]

These reflections, as well as doubts harbored by most thoughtful people, indicate to a small degree how complicating to simple living television can be. A random listing of the complexities resulting from television may well give one pause.

*Advertising*—Choices are made on the basis of the sophisticated hard sell. Christians do well to learn to evaluate, to spot slanting, to resist hidden persuaders.

*Time spent in television viewing*—The hours dedicated to television can seriously impede family communications. Children's learning to enjoy reading is diminished.

*Morals and behavior models*—As presented on television, these are generally extremely different from the standards held by Christian families. Christians need to exercise control of which programs are viewed and vigorously speak up about unworthy programs.

*Effects of television on children*—Many studies are available which look into the effects of violence on young viewers. Also, children need physical activity more than many passive hours planted before the tube.

*Effects on the churches*—Many hail the religious programs of television as being a most effective medium to spread the gospel. Others insist that since the gospel must be mediated by the witness of person to person, life to life, and heart to heart, television cannot be a substitute.

Television is one of many facets of culture having enormous effect on values and life-style. The thoughtful believer will seek help in the battle to achieve a balance between the culture and Christian principles. The best source of aid is a careful and constant immersion in the study and application of the teachings of the Bible. Reflection, prayer, commitment, and action based on the biblical model are essential tools. Discussions with peers and respected Christian leaders can help develop awareness and standards for evaluation.

Although television is a dramatic illustration of the struggle for escape from culture, there are other traps. The current emphasis on the rights of the individual without consideration for the welfare of the group is a serious matter. One course of action would involve a retreat from individualism gone rampant and a return to building communities which are based on enlightened self-interest. This means ensuring neighborhoods that are safe and providing jobs to assure the dignity of all persons. Such actions would mean a retreat from the current bent for learning assertiveness, doing one's own thing, and finding oneself.

A significant aberration in American culture today is the rise in numbers of people joining religious cults and sects. Perhaps the selective expressions of *some* Christian values by these groups is the enticement for troubled youth and unhappy adults. Every community knows of persons who have been separated from their families by the strong attachments to one or another cult group. Such defections dramatize the need for Christians to select and define the culture which they wish to transmit to the next generation. Such division of families is but another of the complicating factors of modern life which makes us yearn for and desire a simpler life-style.

In the literature of our culture, Christians need to heed the words of Deane E. D. Downey. Writing in *Christianity Today,* Downey discusses the avenues of confrontation or escapism as means of dealing with modern literature. Chairman of the Division of Humanities at Trinity Wesleyan College in British Colombia, Canada, Downey discusses the attitude of the Christian toward current writing. His views and the criteria outlined can be applied not only to literature but also to the performing arts and possibly to the plastic arts as well.[7]

Downey addresses the problems faced by the Christian regarding a proper response to "the repugnant realism and feeble moral relativism found in much modern literature."[8] He points out that some Christians choose avoidance but that this may be simply outright escapism. If the Christian is to fulfill his/her task of being salt in the world to season unwholesome society, then a confrontation is a necessity and involvement is required.

According to Downey, "Good literature engages us as whole beings, directing our attention to the awesomeness and the awfulness of the human condition."[9] Downey insists that the believer who wishes to be in touch with the culture must be acquainted with its literature. He notes that modern literature will likely offend the Christian reader by its "incessant realism in depicting various evidences of human depravity—especially physical violence, scurrilous language, or illicit sexuality," and by its "moral relativism, where there seems to be no identifiable criterion for judging human behavior."[10] He proposes that nevertheless one should read modern literature.

The Bible itself does not avoid depicting the full portrait of humankind as sinners. Downey points out that the Bible never glosses over wickedness which is eventually punished. It does imply a solution for sinful persons; evil behavior is treated frankly and succinctly. He concludes that the Christian reader can guide responses to modern literature by trying to ascertain the author's purpose and value system for the portrayal of human depravity, by continually assessing her/his own responses to the material, and by refraining from imposing his own views on others in an indiscriminant manner. Christians must take care about leaving all art and culture totally in the hands of nonbelievers.[11]

Christians can confront the culture which they must transmit to the young in very much the same manner that Jesus taught the eager crowd by the Sea of Galilee. The Christian needs to be far enough from shore for Christian distinctives to be clearly seen. Yet, the believer must be close enough to the world to be heard. By being in tune with current thoughts, she/he will be wise enough to know how to bear witness to the timeless message of God's good news of redemption which is above and beyond all passing cultures.

# Notes

1. Virginia Stem Owens, *The Total Image* (Grand Rapids: William B. Eerdmans Publishing Co., 1980), p. 5.

2. In Lawrence Perrine, *Literature: Structure, Sound and Sense* (New York: Harcourt, Brace & World, 1980), p. 870.

3. Melanie M. Dover, "Readings for Teachers," unpublished paper (Knoxville: University of Tennessee, 1979).

4. Malcolm Muggeridge, *Christ and the Media* (Grand Rapids: William B. Eerdmans Publishing Company, 1977), p. 44.

5. Owens, p. 17.

6. Muggeridge, p. 33.

7. Deane E. D. Downey, "What's Wrong With Reading Modern Literature?" *Christianity Today* (April 8, 1983), pp. 61-62.

8. Ibid, p. 61.

9. Ibid.

10. Ibid.

11. Ibid, p. 62.

# 9

# THE SEARCH FOR PEACE
## The Impact and Pressures of Politics

Politics is the art of managing government and business and other affairs of human beings. This kind of management affects all of us and affects our lives in many significant ways. Persons who have a gift for management and for exercising the art of politics can exercise these gifts to the benefit of the larger group. Politics is a good place for Christians to become involved.

William Lee Miller defines politics as "the fight for power wherever it is."[1] He describes politics as the struggle over decisions on which people differ by groups, the conflict over ability to make decisions and over power.[2]

Political decisions add to the complexity and/or simplicity of modern life. The tangles of relationships among groups and power structures is apparent in all aspects of everyday affairs. The impact and the pressures on the man and woman in the street is heavy and important, too important to be ignored or left to someone (usually anyone) else.

How does a Christian meet this dilemma head-on and become involved without becoming entangled? How can being involved lead to simple living rather than to more complications and problems?

It is apparent that Christians should participate in elections by voting, campaigning, and even running for office. Christians need to express opinions to elected officials; they ought to serve on citizens' committees. These choices have to be carefully made in order to have influence and at the same time preserve a person's allocation of time and energy.

Life is made more complex by the conflicting demands of a pluralistic society. Christians can be drawn into a worship and church involvement which smacks of civil religion. The examples in the New Testament should cause the thoughtful Christian to carefully evaluate his/her own attitudes and expectations about his religion and his/her patriotism to be certain that the meld is not civil religion rather than the living out of the gospel of Jesus Christ.

Thoughtful Christians will examine issues to keep their Christian faith from disintegrating into mere civil religion. Keeping in mind that allegiance to God and to the demands of the gospel is the higher allegiance is a first step to maintaining a distinction between patriotism and religious practice.

There is a temptation to see one's nation as having a preferred status in God's eyes. Scripture teaches that God loved the *world* and sent his son to die for *whosoever* believes. The truth of God's love for everyone was brought home forcefully in the example of a Southern Baptist missionary to the United Nations. Speaking to a seminary chapel service, he asked, "Have you prayed for the president of the Soviet Union today?" Bringing his piercing glance to bear on the faces before him, he reminded the group, "We are enjoined by Scripture to pray for those in authority, for our enemies, as well as our own country and for our friends."

It is easy to confuse love of country with religious emotion. Christians must proceed cautiously. To live the gospel often means being lovingly objective about the system under which we operate. It is well to remind ourselves of the radical view of the Reformation that led Baptists to insist on severe separation of government from religion. Baptist views, positions, and actions in defense of separation of church and state are well known. This generation will do well to review our history and principles and then evaluate carefully our support of current policies in this vital area of community life.

Religious pluralism confuses and deflects us from serving Christ. We can spend so much time on theological hair splitting that we leave undone those things which we ought to do. It is better to be Christ to those who do not know him, to be servant to those inside the church, to be redemptive to those outside the church, than to be fluent in philosophy and apologetics.

The Christian is often found in a state of tension as he/she makes choices. This is true in the area of civil and religious practices and policies. It is a precarious balancing act to be a good citizen and at the same time remain the believer who deliberately places allegiance to God first—ahead of all other loyalties. Paul the apostle wrote of being in submission to government, but he also pointed out that his message of wisdom to the spiritually mature "is not the wisdom that belongs to this world or to the powers that rule this world—powers that are losing their power" (1 Cor. 2:6, GNB). The tension is there; the choices are to be made.

Politics and managing differences among groups in a pluralistic society is extremely important in providing freedom for exercise of simplicity. Another area which demands the attention of the Christian is the concern for peace, both peace in the world and in the inner spirit of the individual. Wise and thoughtful people have observed that the issue of nuclear war—the issue of world peace—may be the *only* issue before humankind.

This generation is the first that gets so much knowledge and culture directly—without culture being filtered through the parents, grandparents, institutions. The impact of this immediacy creates a mental attitude very different from the attitudes of previous generations. Couple these vast differences with the modern American emphasis on the individual, and one can begin to see the sources of so much of the turmoil in our society. There is a scarcity of inner, personal peace. There is too little group and institutional concord.

The Christian can search and work for inner peace, peace with other persons, and peace with God. An example of this peace is the Congregational minister who turned down opportunities to leave a tiny Appalachian town for grander fields. Brother D. was a gifted, warm, and capable pastor. His excellent ministry called him to the attention of larger and more influential congregations in important cities. He chose to pursue his vocation in the smaller place, to concentrate on developing himself, his family, and the people to whom he preached. After decades of quiet life and work, to be in his company was to be at peace. His inner peace communicated itself to those with whom he talked. He was a true reconciler—a man at peace with God, with himself, and with others.

The broader community is a viable place for Christians to

make the impact of politics in the best sense. No vacuum exists in which one can practice Christianity; it must be exercised in the world as it is. Virginia Owens says, "Human creations never take place in a sterile vacuum but in an atmosphere heavy with the germs of culture, the shared perceptions of an age. Although the work of an artist may be solitary, it represents the possibilities available to humanity at that particular time and place."[3]

Care must be taken to not merely become imitators of the culture in which we live. Owens goes on to say, "At best we Christians are currently poor imitators of the cultural productions of our society."[4] "A summons to free the captive vision of Christ's people from the constricting notion that what we are involved in is a giant advertising campaign for salvation."[5]

Other avenues for Christians to be the salt of the earth can be found in the public sector of voluntary work. This aspect of American life is unique and makes a positive contribution to the quality of life as talented women and men give of time and effort in a wide variety of activities. Voluntarism reflects the American impulse to serve others, to be good stewards of time and talents, and the willingness to become involved.

The list of volunteer opportunities is limitless. If anyone has no idea of where to volunteer, a call to the local volunteer coordinating agency will provide an extensive list. Local church congregations provide a scope of places for service that can tap into all kinds of skills. This placement of effort is a ministry to human needs which is a strategic arena for being Christ to other persons.

One should not limit thinking of places to volunteer to traditional white collar jobs. Areas such as building maintenance, working on lawns, in clerical positions, in day care, and other areas can stimulate persons looking for places to serve. Gifts and opportunities can be matched for effective ministry.

Spiritual freedom, political freedom, and religious liberty are related conditions; but they are not synonomous or necessarily concomitant conditions. Paul in Roman chains or Bonhoeffer in a Nazi prison suffered both from denial of political freedom and religious liberty, but no two men were ever more free in mind and in spiritual realm.

Paul abided by Roman law willingly, appealing to Caesar for trial on charges of treason against Rome for preaching Christ. Bonhoeffer submitted to prison and to death because his spiritual allegiance went beyond the political organization operating the government of Germany.

In the United States of America today we are unaware of and often ungrateful for this trilogy of the blessings of freedom to which we are heir. Too many Americans fail to exercise these rights which have been dearly bought and bequeathed to us.

Do we exercise spiritual freedom by disciplined, regular, and thoughtful attention to growing in wisdom and understanding of the gospel and of the full impact these teachings should have on our thoughts and actions? Do we regularly exercise our political freedom not only to vote but also to guarantee political rights to others, by standing up for all groups and individuals—especially those whose views differ from ours?

Do we maintain a stance of exercising our religious liberties by practice and participation in our own expression of the church of Jesus Christ? Do we remain vigilant in concern and action on the behalf of all people to have the liberty to practice (or not to practice) religion, knowing that they and we are accountable only to God?

Jesus said, "Know the truth, and the truth shall make you free" (John 8:32). Knowing the truth of Christ guarantees true spiritual freedom. He also said, "Render therefore unto Caesar, . . ." indicating our obligation to the political government of our society, but he also admonished us to render "unto God the things that are God's" (Matt. 22:21). We are to know the truth and to be spiritually free.

Our English forebears handed us a laboriously achieved political liberty which they claimed as the right of every man. Our American founding fathers established this government on the strong basis that government has no right to interfere in a person's relationship with God. As Americans, and as Christians, we have an obligation to seize our liberties, to not only *say* but to *demonstrate* with our lives that "In God We Trust." When we do these things, we will have availed ourselves of three great blessings: spiritual freedom, political freedom, and religious liberty.

# Notes

1. William Lee Miller, *The Protestant and Politics* (Philadelphia: The Westminster Press, 1958), p. 17.

2. Ibid, p. 17.

3. Virginia Stem Owens, *The Total Image* (Grand Rapids: William B. Eerdmans Publishing Co., 1980), p. 10.

4. Ibid.

5. Ibid, p. 11.

# 10

# THE SEARCH FOR SIMPLICITY

## The Need for Simple Living

Almost everyone will agree that at least some changes need to be made in his/her life. Many will readily admit that they need to take charge and set priorities that are in keeping with Christian principles. All of us long to emulate the model of our servant-Lord, our simple-living Savior with his robe and sandals and minimum of amenities. The question which overwhelms us is, "How can I take charge? Where do I begin?" This book will be of little worth unless suggestions are made and followed.

The author and the reader can begin to live more simply by first of all *deciding* to do something. Then the steps are clear: have a plan, set attainable goals, decide on priorities, on a day at an hour begin. It is essential to keep in mind that the changes won't be easy; there will be failures, discouragement, backsliding. The person pursuing simple living will need to begin again and again. One must realize that the battle is never totally won, and victory over greed, selfishness, laziness, and gluttony is never total in this life.

To pursue a path to simple living and to develop the gift for simplicity which lies within each of us, we must consider the objections. To live more simply is not to turn back the clock; nor is it a means of escaping reality. To argue that abandoning materialism as a high priority is a negative and possibly destructive move is shortsighted. Gabriel Marcel has well said that "the only way to rediscover the path to the sacral is to turn away from the world and recapture simplicity, which is perhaps only another word for uniqueness and inwardness, *the* favorite abode of the sacral." The sacral and the simple have affinity. Simple living will nourish the sacral in daily life.

Claiming the gift of simplicity and developing the gift are steps toward freedom. To move from complexity to simplicity requires effort and it *is* a struggle. This struggle and search are well worth the pain and the discipline. Once a discipline of simplicity is adopted, we can enjoy the freedom which is its fruit.

Carlyle Marney asserted that the Christian is conscious of "belonging to a higher community. Christians know this community as the kingdom of God and say that the source and ground of Christian ethics is here . . . so he longs for the kingdom of God and rebels against the confinement of his provincialism and stands with his chest against the fence wanting freedom to seek this beatitude of universal love on his own."[2]

Once we get down to basics and decide to develop the characteristics which result in simple Christian living, we begin the struggle. An action plan can have some of the following components:

> deciding what we *need;*
> discovering what we *want;*
> describing what we *hope.*

We must keep before us the realization that what we often have is:

    complexity and bondage;
    little control of our own time;
    stresses and distresses;
    fears and anxieties;
    guilt and resentment;
    doubts and spiritual poverty.

To counter these negatives we can act by

    taking control;
    establishing priorities;
    setting goals;
    defining a definite plan;
    beginning, sticking to our plan;
    having courage to try again when we falter.

Simplicity is a matter of putting first things first. Power for this comes from right relationship with God. Having things in proper order brings freedom, simple living, good relationships with others, and respect for the environment. Such attitudes aid us, as the Shaker hymn says, "to come down where we ought to be." Joyfully we can dwell in a "garden of delights." Eden? Yes. Impossible? Maybe. Worth the search? Absolutely.

Some reasons for thoughtful persons to consider establishing a simple life-style have been proposed by Jorgen Lissner of the Lutheran World Federation. He suggests that:

> A simpler lifestyle is not a panacea. It may be embarked upon for the wrong reasons, e.g., out of guilt, as a substitute for political action, or in quest for moral purity. But

it can also be meaningful and significant in some or all of these ways. . . .

1. As an *act of faith,* done for the sake of personal integrity and as an expression of personal commitment to a more equitable distribution of the world's wealth.

2. As an *act of self-defense* against the mind- and body-polluting effects of overconsumption.

3. As an *act of withdrawal* from the achievement-neurosis of our high-pressure materialist societies.

4. As an *act of solidarity* with the majority of human-kind, which has no choice about life-styles.

5. As an *act of sharing* with others what has been given to us, or of returning what was usurped by us through unjust social and economic systems.

6. As an *act of celebration* of the riches found in creativity, spirituality, and community with others, in place of mindless materialism.

7. As an *act of provocation* (ostentatious *under*con-sumption) to arouse curiosity leading to dialogue with others about affluence, alienation, poverty, and social injustice.

8. As an *act of anticipation* of the era when the under-privileged will force new power relationships and new patterns of resource allocation upon us.

9. As an *act of advocacy* of legislated changes in present patterns of production and consumption, in the direction of a new international economic order.

10. As an *exercise of purchasing power* to redirect pro-duction away from the satisfaction of artificially created wants toward the supply of goods and services that meet genuine social needs.[3]

There are as many ways to live simply as there are people. The following stories are about real persons who have chosen to take at least one step toward simplicity. It may seem, on the surface, to be an insignificant step. The action may appear trivial and of no possible aid to developing the gift of simplicity. However, if we will consider these steps, we can see that everyone can begin to do something. Many people are habitual practicers of some aspect of simple living. We can all continue those habits which lead to simple living and decide upon others which will fit into our aims.

Nell tells of a practice she recently adopted. Having read of how much more grain it takes to produce a pound of beef, she decided she would concentrate on poultry and fish in her own kitchen. She has decided to do this quietly, without fanfare or seeking attention. "It may just be a little help in doing something specific about world hunger."

Amanda and her husband are exerting self-discipline in plain living in several ways. "We determined to live simply in retirement," she says. First, they built a modest, two-bedroom, one-bath home. Next, they determined to make do with one automobile, even though both have many activities and engagements.

Some more intense persons are experimenting with raising the family's food on small plots through intensive farming. Others go a step further and raise vegetables without commercial fertilizer and without chemical pesticides. It is possible that such courageous pioneers will be able to teach others by their example. Perhaps our children will take up these practices to the benefit of their families and their health.

Seminary students have been known to come away from rallies supporting meeting the needs of the hungry in the world with determination to change their own life-style.

One couple, after hearing the facts about world hunger, sought the help of a nutritionist. With expert guidance these young people changed the way they shopped for groceries, selected their food, prepared it, and ate it. After a few months of such intense study and dedicated action, they found the regimen good in several ways. Not only had they changed their life-style to benefit others, but they also looked better. Each had lost unwanted pounds, so that they looked better, felt better, and had an improved attitude toward themselves.

More and more there are stories surfacing of church congregations who decide on changes that lead to simple living. One congregation set the goal in a fund-raising campaign to include money for a specific project on a specific mission field. Such action will cause churches to evaluate their own building needs more wisely and to broaden real concern beyond the immediate community. To have needs of others clearly before us will cause us to be more modest in our outlay on our own concerns.

Both men and women are searching for ways to earn a living which will leave enough time for family, church, community, and other personal concerns. One highly trained young woman arranged to continue her work at home. This allowed her to be with her three children, continue to earn money, and to keep abreast of her highly technical field. People who have certain skills can look at this possibility and make preparation for a drastically different life-style.

Other professionals find that taking a long break from their hectic schedules can bring about a deliberate change in life-style. One couple, both of whom are teachers, enjoyed a brief sabbatical filled with time for walks, reading, and a careful reassessment of life goals and life activities. The two decided to lower long-range ambitions in favor of more time together and more time for creative activities.

There are still scores of young men and young women in our society who choose to serve rather than setting their sights on making money and getting ahead. One such young woman was reminded that she could make twice as much money in an occupation she was qualified for than in the teaching she was doing. She responded to this suggestion rather tartly. "I know I could make more money, but that is not what I have set out to do. I want to teach because I want to serve. It is a choice I am consciously making."

One young man of great talents decided on the trade of carpentry. He was aware that the maximum in earnings would be reached early in his working years. The satisfaction of making something with his hands outweighed the prospects of other careers for him. He made an informed decision to live more simply, to work more physically, but to have the satisfaction that comes only to the skilled craftsman when he beholds the work of his hands, knowing he has created something useful.

Electing to avoid the keeping up with the Joneses syndrome often takes careful planning. One young adult couple decided to live in less house than they could afford, drive a more modest car than they could buy, to keep their wants below what they could pay for. This kind of life-style affords them peace of mind as well as leaving more margin in their budget for money to give away.

Others take charge of their life and their time in careful choices of scheduling. One man whose job requires a great deal of travel is careful to arrange his itinerary so that he can have adequate time for family, friends, and church. Grady Nutt, the late Southern Baptist humorist and speaker, always made it a point to be in town on Sunday and in his church. His example has already been a significant influence on scores of young people. To keep personal goals in a proper balance is not easy, especially for gifted persons who are in great demand. The exercise of the gift of simplicity in such persons takes determination and careful planning. It can be done, and it is most effective when it is.

In times of great stress or when a person is suffering from worry and depression, there are actions to take. To simplify life in these times of suffering, one young mother began to make bread. She learned to knead, to use different grains, to make large quantities. The effort she put into the preparation and the baking proved to be healing in her own soul. Another woman in her midyears found that long, brisk walks restored her peace of mind and defused her irritable spirit. Such exercise made it possible for her to deal with a difficult family situation with greater calm and more patience.

A help to start the search is in the Shakertown Pledge which was drafted some years ago at a conference at Shakertown in Pleasant Hill, Kentucky. The people who drew up the pledge wish it to be freely and widely distributed. It is included here for you to consider.

## The Shakertown Pledge

Recognizing that the earth and the fulness thereof is a gift from our gracious God, and that we are called to cherish, nurture, and provide loving stewardship for the earth's resources, and recognizing that life itself is a gift, and a call to responsibility, joy, and celebration, I make the following declarations:

1. I declare myself to be a world citizen.
2. I commit myself to lead an ecologically sound life.
3. I commit myself to lead a life of creative simplicity and to share my personal wealth with the world's poor.
4. I commit myself to join with others in the reshaping of institutions in order to bring about a more just global society in which all people have full access to the needed resources for their physical, emotional, intellectual, and spiritual growth.
5. I commit myself to occupational accountability, and in so doing I will seek to avoid the creation of products which cause harm to others.
6. I affirm the gift of my body and commit myself to its proper nourishment and physical well-being.
7. I commit myself to examine continually my relations with others, and to attempt to relate honestly, morally, and lovingly to those around me.
8. I commit myself to personal renewal through prayer, meditation, and study.
9. I commit myself to responsible participation in a community of faith.[4]

# Notes

1. Gabriel Marcel, *Searchings* (New York: Newman Press, 1967), p. 52.

2. Carlyle Marney, *Structures of Prejudice* (New York: Abingdon Press, 1961), pp. 117-118.

3. John V. Taylor, *Enough Is Enough* (Minneapolis: Augsburg Publishing House, 1977), pp. 121-122.

4. Adam Daniel Finnerty, *No More Plastic Jesus: Global Justice and Christian Lifestyle* (Maryknoll, New York: Orbis Books, 1977), p. 97.

# Epilogue

I am convinced that the search for simplicity is a definite response to make and a positive action to take. We must move to loosen the bonds that enslave us to the least attractive aspects of modern society. The believer must do some serious thinking, decide on appropriate goals, plan a workable program, and then have the determination to keep on trying.

Peace, inner peace, is one major goal. Like Gulliver, we are bound down. Just as he was restrained and rendered impotent by the scores of Lilliputians, each of us allows the demands of others to bind us. We are held down by what we think others expect of us. But we have the liberating words of the gospel. Our lives should radiate joy and power, not grimness and weakness. The ability to overcome and to endure is available to us. This joy comes from inner peace occasioned by life lived more thoughtfully. We need to live lives characterized by a slower pace and unencumbered by excessive possessions. A more peaceful, a more simple existence can be achieved. To do this we must take seriously the example of Jesus of Nazareth and choose to follow his way.

Too often we let the standards of the culture around us make us "of the world" as we live our lives "in the world." It does not have to be this way. To claim the gift of simplicity and to begin the search for a simple life-style takes courage and determination. Courage is needed because it goes against the human tendency toward satisfying greed. Greediness has been legitimatized by the ideals of the free enterprise system. The appeal of laissez-faire economics to the human need or inclination to accumulate mitigates against simple living. Determination is needed to offset our desire for instant results. It is hard to remain satisfied with slow progress.

Almost everything in modern life tends toward the bondage of complexity: use of time, management of money, stressful living, and the culture itself in which we live. Life is further complicated by the impact of the media on all aspects of society. We are tangled up in our emotional relationships as well as by the effects of politics and economics on our values and priorities. Overlaying all these knotty problems is the modern climate of religious agnosticism and scientific secularization of life. We are living in a time of rapidly changing mores, morals, and values. Change occurs so rapidly that we are whirled about in a state of unending dizziness.

We are literally bombarded with persuasion and propaganda from every side. It is no wonder that we feel as jerked about as the last person in a game of crack the whip!

It is imperative that Christians take time to review the teachings of the Bible and the example of Jesus. With these measures for our daily life, we can take careful estimate of the bondage which restrains our joy in living. We can see the battle lines. Then we know that there are principles to apply. There are steps to take. There is a day to say, "I will begin to search for a simple manner of living." There is a gift to claim, to recognize, to develop.

By search and struggle, we can claim the gift of simplicity and begin to be more nearly free. The joy and peace which will result are worth the time, the effort, the hardship, and the pain. We can come into a full realization of the dream of what the simple Christian life can be. We can set limits for our involvement. These limits can describe what we will commit ourselves to do and to be. Then we will begin to see in our lives the fruits of the Spirit. Paul enumerated these fruits which we all desire: "love, joy, peace, patience, kindness, goodness, faithfulness, humility, and self-control" (Gal. 5:22, GNB).

Then we will have searched for and struggled to claim the simple life. We will incorporate into our families the gift of simplicity. Then we will see that simple living is truly Christian living.

New Testament passages which deal with simple living include 1 Peter 3:3-4, GNB, in which Peter admonished women to not depend on outward aids to beauty. "Instead, your beauty should consist of your true inner self, the ageless beauty of a gentle and quiet spirit, which is of the greatest value in God's sight." These words can be applied with equal force to the male Christians. A gentle and quiet spirit is very descriptive of Jesus and thus a model for men and women who wish to be like him.

Some observations make a point that needs no elaboration: Jesus had one robe and had no place to lay his head. The early Christians as described in Acts shared all they had, putting no premium on who had more or less of the world's goods. Paul accepted support from various churches, worked at tent making, and seemed to seek only enough to meet basic needs. We are told to eat and drink to the glory of God. Applying that admonition should affect what and how much we eat and drink! The entire epistle of James has clear teachings on how we value money, how we treat rich and poor, and just what pure religion is.

The prophets in the Old Testament preach to the rich and the fat, pointing out that too often they have amassed their wealth by exploiting the poor. This question of justice is worth a study all its own. For our purposes, it is enough to point out that God requires caring for the needy, justice for the poor, and sharing by the well-to-do.

In the area of conserving the environment and caring for the earth and its resources, it must be said that many have misinterpreted God's commands in Genesis. When he told the man and woman to dress the earth, he did not mean to exploit and use it up. To dress a garden implies making it productive. A good gardener sees that the soil is fertilized and kept in condition to go on producing. To be the gardener of the earth means to use it for one's own needs and to enrich it to provide for the needs of those who come after. Many are speaking and writing today to cause mankind to look upon the planet earth as a spaceship which must be carefully tended for the benefit of those living today and for the use of those who come after this generation. Simple living is an inextricable part of the efforts to conserve and to enrich the planet for the benefit of those who come after us.

"Then Jesus said to the disciples, 'And so I tell you not to worry about the food you need to stay alive or about the clothes you need for your body. Life is much more important than food, and the body much more important than clothes. Look at the crows: they don't plant seeds or gather a harvest; they don't have storage rooms or barns; God feeds

them! You are worth so much more than birds! Can any of you live a bit longer by worrying about it? If you can't manage even such a small thing, why worry about the other things? Look how the wild flowers grow: they don't work or make clothes for themselves. But I tell you that not even King Solomon with all his wealth had clothes as beautiful as one of these flowers. It is God who clothes the wild grass— grass that is here today and gone tomorrow, burned up in the oven. Won't he be all the more sure to clothe you? What little faith you have! So don't be all upset, always concerned about what you will eat and drink. (For the pagans of this world are always concerned about all these things.) Your Father knows that you need these things. Instead, be concerned with his Kingdom, and he will provide you with these things.'"
(Luke 12:22-31, GNB)

"And God is able to give you more than you need, so that you will always have all you need for yourselves and more than enough for every good cause. As the scripture says, 'He gives generously to the needy; his kindness lasts forever.' And God, who supplies seed for the sower and bread to eat, will also supply you with all the seed you need and will make it grow and produce a rich harvest from your generosity. He will always make you rich enough to be generous at all times, so that many will thank God for your gifts which they receive from us."
(2 Cor. 9:8-11, GNB)

Let us be doers of the Word! Let us begin to search for the simple life and to develop the gift of simplicity.

# For Further Thought and Discussion

## Chapter 1

1.   Describe the top five priorities for pioneer families of one hundred years ago.
2.   List the top five priorities for families today.
3.   How do these two lists compare? Are they more alike or more different?
4.   Make a diary of your family's activities for a week. Evaluate the diary to see if first things get first place in your schedule.
5.   Select some of the questions in this chapter's litany for your own thought and review.

## Chapter 2

1.   Using the definitions for simplicity in this chapter, write out your definition for a simple life-style for you and your family.
2.   Spend time thinking over Richard Foster's ten principles for simple living. How can you apply these principles to your life-style?
3.   What are some advantages for the Christian to begin to demonstrate more of a simple life-style?

4. Recall and describe Christians you know who live model simple life-styles.
5. What additional Scriptures teach simple living? List.

## Chapter 3

1. Define *success*. How does your definition relate to Christian ideals in attitude and behavior?
2. Discuss the benefits and dangers of a competitive attitude.
3. List three situations where the rights of the individual and the rights of the group are in conflict.
4. How can a Christian resolve these conflicts?
5. Discuss the particular ways one-parent families find life more complex.
6. How can other Christians help such families?
7. Do we have sumptuary laws today? Should we? If so, what kind?

## Chapter 4

1. Discuss Grubbs's idea of having "fewness of wants" and "reasonableness of wants."
2. To what extent do we need possessions to have basic happiness?
3. Can we have simplicity in material things and still enjoy beauty in objects? If so, how? Is this desirable?
4. Discuss possible reasons for the unhappy affluent people described by Walker Percy. Do these reasons and situations affect you? How?
5. Give careful thought to the Bible's teachings about

covetousness. Read other Bible passages on this topic.
How does all this relate to your life-style?

6.    Discuss the "reasons for Christians to spend less" and
      "to earn more." Do these reasons reflect Christian
      principles? Will the application reflect a simplified
      life-style?

7.    List ways advertising influences your choices.

## Chapter 5

1.    Evaluate how you apportion your time.

2.    How much time do you spend in work, leisure, helping
      others, attending church, being with family and
      friends?

3.    Is your time spent in ways you feel are important?

4.    How would you re-allocate your day if you could do
      exactly as you please?

5.    Do you have an hour a week for study, prayer, and
      personal growth? More than an hour? Less? Are you
      pleased with the time set apart for these activities?

## Chapter 6

1.    Do you say, "I love you" to someone every day?

2.    How do you cope with strong negative feelings such as
      fear, anger, and guilt?

3.    Do you agree or disagree with the idea of loving your-
      self second only to loving God?

4.    Do you spiritually nurture yourself? How?

5.    Do you have at least two close friends?

6.    Define what a close friend is.

7. To what extent do you attempt to make decisions for other people?
8. In what ways do you depend on other people to give significance to what you do?
9. To what extent are you self-reliant?
10. Reflect on Galatians 5:22. How can you go about developing these fruits of the Spirit in your life?

## Chapter 7

1. Take the Stress Test developed at Boston University Medical Center.
2. What steps should you take toward changing your life-style as a result of this test?
3. Is it desirable to live without any stress? Why? Why not?
4. How can Christians develop life-styles to help one another deal with stress?
5. How can teachings from the Bible help Christians to live with less stress and tension?

## Chapter 8

1. Why should a Christian strive to be IN but not OF the world?
2. What are some principles a Christian can use in deciding on what is worldly?
3. How are you transmitting your beliefs to your children and/or the younger generation?
4. List five traditions we can use to pass on truths to the next generation.

5.  How can the churches transmit Christian beliefs without being caught in the inflexibility of traditions?
6.  What are some ways to evaluate movies and books?
7.  What are the dangers of Christians withdrawing too far from the culture in which they live?
8.  What are the dangers of being too closely identified with the practices of the society in which we live?

## Chapter 9

1.  How does the Christian balance participation in politics with being separated from the world?
2.  Should Christians become involved in the power struggles of politics? Why? Why not?
3.  Does involvement in politics make simple living impossible? Why?
4.  What is civil religion?
5.  Does civil religion simplify or complicate life-style?
6.  Is volunteer work in any sense political?
7.  Do you believe that Christians should be community volunteers?
8.  To what extent do Christians avail themselves of the freedoms we enjoy in the United States?

## Chapter 10

1.  Write out changes in your life-style which you wish to make.
2.  Develop a simple timetable to achieve at least one change in your life-style that will simplify.
3.  Reflect on the expected results of your goal once it is attained.

4. Will your change exhibit any of the characteristics listed by Jorgen Lissner?

5. Do you already practice some traits of simple living?

6. Write down the elements of a simple life-style which you now practice.

7. List ways you can further simplify.

8. Study the Shakertown Pledge.

9. Which parts of the pledge can you subscribe to at this time?

10. Draft a description of the manner in which Jesus worked and lived. Would you describe his life-style as simple? What elements of his manner of living can you emulate?

# Bibliography

Burns, David. *Feeling Good: The New Mood Therapy.* New York: William Morrow, quoted in "Think Your Way Out of Depression," *The Reader's Digest,* December 1980.

Cream, Davis, and Ebbeson, Eric and Helen. *Living Simply: An Examination of Christian Lifestyles.* New York: The Seabury Press, 1981.

Downey, Deane E. D. "What's Wrong with Reading Modern Literature?" *Christianity Today,* April 8, 1983.

Dover, Melanie McEwen. "Readings for Teachers," unpublished master's program paper. University of Tennessee at Knoxville, 1979.

Easterlin, Richard A. "Does Money Buy Happiness?" *Economics: A Reader.* Ed. Kenneth G. Elzinga. New York: Harper and Row, 1975.

Elgin, Duane. *Voluntary Simplicity.* New York: William Morrow, 1981.

Eliot, T. S. "Burnt Norton," *The Four Quartets.* New York: Harcourt, Brace and World, 1943.

Finnerty, Adam Daniel. *No More Plastic Jesus: Global Justice and Christian Lifestyle.* Maryknoll, New York: Orbis Books, 1977.

*Good News Bible: Today's English Version*. New York: American Bible Society, 1976.

Grubbs, Edward A. *Social Aspects of the Quaker Faith*. London: Headly Brothers, 1899.

Hoye, Ida Jayne. "The Legacy of Horatio Alger," *The Chattanooga News-Free Press* (Dec. 4, 1983), J-7.

LeShan, Lawrence, and Margenau, Henry. *Einstein's Space and Van Gogh's Sky*. New York: Macmillan Company, 1982.

Marcel, Gabriel. *Searchings*. New York: Newman Press, 1967.

Marney, Carlyle. *Structures of Prejudice*. New York: Abingdon Press, 1961.

Marvell, Andrew. "To His Coy Mistress," *The Poem: An Anthology*. Ed. Green, Stanley B., and Weatherhead, A. Kingsley. New York: Appleton-Century-Crofts, 1968.

Miller, William Lee. *The Protestant and Politics*. Philadelphia: The Westminster Press, 1958.

Muggeridge, Malcolm. *Christ and the Media*. Grand Rapids: William B. Eerdmans, 1977.

Nalley, Richard V. "The Simple Shaker Style," *US AIR* (June 1983), 42-60.

Owens, Virginia Stem. *The Total Image*. Grand Rapids: William B. Eerdmans, 1980.

Peck, M. Scott. *The Road Less Traveled*. New York: Simon and Schuster, 1978.

Percy, Walker. *The Message in the Bottle*. New York: Farrar, Straus and Giroux, 1980.

Perrine, Lawrence. *Literature: Structure, Sound and Sense*. New York: Harcourt, Brace and World, 1980.

Scott, Dru. *How To Put More Time Into Your Life*. New York: Rawson Wade Publishers, 1980.

Selye, Hans. *Stress Without Distress.* New York: J. B. Lippincott, 1974.

Shakespeare, William. "Sonnet LX," *Shakespeare's Sonnets.* Ed. Hyder E. Rollins. New York: Appleton-Century-Crofts, 1951.

"Stress: Can We Cope?" *Time,* CXXI (June 6, 1983), 48-54.

"Sumptuary Laws," *The New Encyclopedia Britannica,* 1983, 669.

Taylor, John V. *Enough Is Enough.* Minneapolis: Augsburg Publishing House, 1977.

*The American Heritage Dictionary of the English Language.* Ed. William Morris. Boston: American Heritage Publishing Co., 1969.

*Thorndike Barnhart Comprehensive Desk Dictionary.* Garden City: Doubleday, 1969.

Viscott, David. *The Language of Feelings.* New York: Pocket Books, 1976.